System Center 2012 R2 Configuration Manager
A Practical Handbook for Reporting

Steve Thompson

PUBLISHED BY
Deployment Artist
http://deploymentartist.com

Warning and Disclaimer

Every effort has been made to make this book as complete and as accurate as possible, but no warranty or fitness is implied. The information provided is on an "as is" basis. The authors and the publisher shall have neither liability nor responsibility to any person or entity with respect to any loss or damages arising from the information contained in this book.

Feedback Information

We'd like to hear from you! If you have any comments about how we could improve the quality of this book, please don't hesitate to contact us by visiting http://deploymentartist.com, sending an email to feedback@deploymentartist.com, or visiting our Facebook site facebook.com/DeploymentArtist.

Acknowledgements

Writing a book is a serious commitment of time and energy. This work would not be possible without support from my wife, who had to do *even more* while this book was in progress. Thanks to both Ronni Pedersen and Sherri Kissinger for both saying yes when I asked whether I could use their contributions in the book. Thank you, Johan Arwidmark, for asking me to take this project and for your review of this material, while likely deploying the latest version of Windows. ☺ A big thank you to the MVPs and technical community for your sharing of information and collaboration.

About the Author

Steve Thompson is now in his 20th year as an MVP and has developed numerous applications, honing his skills on SQL Server development and client/server applications. With a background in SQL Server, as DBA and advocate for SQL Server technology, Steve started working with Systems Management Server when it was a v1.1 release. Currently, he works for Softchoice Corporation as a Senior Consultant specializing in System Center products.

First awarded MVP in Microsoft Access in Dec 1995, Steve transitioned into SQL Server as an MVP for a few years before joining the System Center team as a Configuration Manager MVP. He is a contributing author for *System Center 2012 Configuration Manager Unleashed* (SAMS) and an advocate for *reporting*! An experienced speaker, he has presented at numerous Microsoft Management Summit, IT / Dev Connections, and TechEd events, and at numerous other conferences.

Contents

Introduction

System Center 2012 R2 Configuration Manager: A Practical Handbook for Reporting is the ultimate collection of resources for the working IT Pro who wants to create and customize reports for Configuration Manager 2012 R2.

Say Hello (Possibly Again) to ViaMonstra Inc.

In this book, you customize reporting for the fictive ViaMonstra Inc. organization. ViaMonstra is a midsized company with a single location and 6500 employees. Its site is located in New York, and the company is using Configuration Manager 2012 R2 for its system management solution.

BTW, the name ViaMonstra comes from *Viam Monstra*, Latin, meaning "Show me the way."

How to Use This Book

I have packed this book with step-by-step guides, which means you build your solution as you read along.

In numbered steps, I have set all names and paths in bold typeface. I also have used a standard naming convention throughout the book when explaining what to do in each step. The steps normally are something like this:

1. On the **Advanced Properties** page, select the **Confirm** check box, and then click **Next**.

Sample scripts are formatted like the following example, on a grey background.

```
DoNotCreateExtraPartition=YES
MachineObjectOU=ou=Workstations,dc=corp,dc=viamonstra,dc=com
```

Code and commands that you type in the guides are displayed like this:

1. Install **MDT 2013** by running the following command in an elevated **PowerShell** prompt:

```
& msiexec.exe /i 'C:\Setup\MDT 2013\
MicrosoftDeploymentToolkit2013_x64.msi' /quiet
```

The step-by-step guides in this book assume that you have configured the environment according to the information in Chapter 1, "ViaMonstra Inc. and the Proof-of-Concept Environment," and in Appendix A.

Sample Files

All sample files used in this book can be downloaded from http://deploymentfundamentals.com.

Additional Resources

In addition to all tips and tricks provided in this book, you can find extra resources like articles and video recordings on my blog, https://stevethompsonmvp.wordpress.com.

Chapter 1

ViaMonstra Inc. and the Proof-of-Concept Environment

As you remember from the introduction, ViaMonstra Inc. is the fictive company I use throughout this book. In this chapter, I describe the company in more detail, as well as the proof-of-concept environment I use in the step-by-step guides. Detailed installation instructions on how to set up the initial environment can be found in Appendix A.

ViaMonstra Inc.

ViaMonstra Inc. was invented for the very purpose of having a "real" company for which to build a deployment solution. These deployment solutions come from multiple real-world consulting engagements I have done, consolidating them into a single generic scenario.

ViaMonstra has 6500 employees and a single location in New York.

Servers

The New York site has the following servers related to software distribution and other supporting infrastructure. All servers are running Windows Server 2012 R2. Detailed configuration of each server is found in the "Servers (Detailed Information)" section in this chapter:

- **DC01.** Domain Controller, DNS, and DHCP
- **CM01.** Member Server

Friendly Reminder: Detailed step-by-step guidance on how to deploy the servers used in the book can be found in Appendix A.

Clients

In addition to the servers, you have two Windows 7 SP1 clients, and two Windows 8.1 clients that you use for testing. As with the servers, Appendix A helps you deploy these machines.

- **PC0001.** Windows 7 SP1 Enterprise x64 client
- **PC0002.** Windows 7 SP1 Enterprise x64 client
- **PC0003.** Windows 8.1 Enterprise x64 client
- **PC0004.** Windows 8.1 Enterprise x64 client

Internet Access

The guides in this book do not require that you to have Internet access on the virtual machines, but if you want to, I recommend using either a virtual router (running in a VM) to provide Internet access to your lab and test VMs, or enabling Internet Connection Sharing (ICS) on the host. If you go the virtual router approach, you can use either the Vyatta / VyOS (Vyatta community fork) routers, or a Windows Server 2012 R2 virtual machine with routing configured.

Note: For detailed guidance on setting up a virtual router for your lab environment, see this article: http://tinyurl.com/usingvirtualrouter.

Software

The following list describes the various applications used by ViaMonstra. To be able to follow all the step-by-step guides and configurations in the book, the following software must be downloaded. They can be either trial or full versions.

- Windows Assessment and Deployment Toolkit (ADK) 8.1
- Configuration Manager 2012 R2
- Configuration Manager 2012 R2 CU4
- SQL Server 2012 Standard SP1
- SQL Server 2012 SP1 CU8
- Windows 7 SP1 Enterprise x64
- Windows 8.1 Enterprise x64
- Windows Server 2012 R2
- SQL Server 2012 Report Builder

Servers (Detailed Information)

As mentioned earlier in this chapter, I'm using a set of servers in my environment. I use a concept called *hydration* (automated build of entire labs and production environments) when creating the servers.

Also as mentioned earlier, for detailed step-by-step guidance on how to deploy the servers, please review Appendix A, "Using the Hydration Kit to Build the PoC Environment."

To set up a virtual environment with all the servers and clients, you need a host with at least 16 GB of RAM, even though 32 GB RAM is recommended. Either way, make sure you are using SSD drives for your storage. A single 480 GB SSD is enough to run all the scenarios in this book.

> **Real World Note:** If using a laptop or desktop when doing the step-by-step guides in this book, please do use a SSD drive for your virtual machines. Using normal spindle-based disks are just too slow for decent lab and test environments. Also please note that most laptops support at least 16 GB of RAM these days, even if many vendors do not update their specifications with this information.

Detailed descriptions of the servers follow:

- **DC01.** A **Windows Server 2012 R2** machine, fully patched with the latest security updates and configured as Active Directory Domain Controller, DNS Server, and DHCP Server in the **corp.viamonstra.com** domain.
    - Server name: **DC01**
    - IP Address: **192.168.1.200**
    - Roles: **DNS, DHCP,** and **Domain Controller**

- **CM01.** A **Windows Server 2012 R2** machine, fully patched with the latest security updates and configured as a member server in the **corp.viamonstra.com** domain. This is the server where you install SQL Server 2012 SP1 and Configuration Manager 2012 R2.
    - Server name: **CM01**
    - IP Address: **192.168.1.214**
    - Roles: **IIS**

Clients (Detailed Information)

In addition to the servers, you also use four clients in the step-by-step guides. The required client virtual machines are the following:

- **PC0001.** A **Windows 7 SP1 Enterprise x64** machine, fully patched with the latest security updates and configured as a member in the **corp.viamonstra.com** domain.
    - Client name: **PC0001**
    - IP Address: **192.168.1.11**
    - Software: **SQL Server 2012 SP1 Tools** and **SQL Server 2012 Report Builder**.

- **PC0002.** A **Windows 7 SP1 Enterprise x64** machine, fully patched with the latest security updates and configured as a member in the **corp.viamonstra.com** domain.
    - Client name: **PC0002**
    - IP Address: **192.168.1.12**

- **PC0003.** A **Windows 8.1 Enterprise x64** machine, fully patched with the latest security updates and configured as a member in the **corp.viamonstra.com** domain.
    - Client name: **PC0003**
    - IP Address: **192.168.1.13**

- **PC0004**. A **Windows 8.1 Enterprise x64** machine, fully patched with the latest security updates and configured as a member in the **corp.viamonstra.com** domain.

  - Client name: **PC0004**

  - IP Address: **192.168.1.14**

Setting Up the Base Configuration Manager 2012 R2 Infrastructure

In this section, you set up a base Configuration Manager 2012 R2 site server. In these guides, you use the CM01 virtual machine you configured as part of the hydration kit. As with Appendix A, most of the setup and configuration is done via script to keep it as automated as possible and, of course, documented.

> **Note:** Explaining all details on why you do the various setup configurations is outside the scope of this Configuration Manager reporting book. But if you want to learn more, I highly recommend reading *System Center 2012 R2 Configuration Manager - Mastering the Fundamentals*, 3rd Edition, by Kent Agerlund. Check this link: http://deploymentartist.com/Books.aspx.

The base configuration involves the following:

- Configure the data disks on CM01

- Install SQL Server 2012 Standard SP1 (including CU8)

- Configure SQL Server memory and database files

- Install Configuration Manager 2012 R2

- Update to Configuration Manager 2012 R2 CU4

- Configure discovery methods (which also creates boundaries)

- Create a boundary group

If you want to run the step-by-step guide in this chapter, you need a lab environment configured as outlined in Appendix A. In this chapter, you use the following virtual machines:

DC01

CM01

The VMs used in this chapter.

You also need to have downloaded the following software:

- The book sample files (http://deploymentfundamentals.com)
- Configuration Manager 2012 R2
- Configuration Manager 2012 R2 CU4
- SQL Server 2012 Standard with SP1
- SQL Server 2012 SP1 CU8

Add Data Disks to CM01

The primary site server for ViaMonstra (CM01) uses six volumes in total: one for the operating system and five for SQL Server and Configuration Manager. If you used the hydration kit to set up CM01, you have only one volume and need to create the additional five.

> **Note:** If you are using Hyper-V, you can use the New-DataDisks-CM01.ps1 script provided in the book sample files to create five data disks and attach them to the CM01 virtual machine.

1. Using either **Hyper-V Manager** or **VMware vSphere**, connect five hard disks / volumes to **CM01** with the following specifications:

    o DataDisk01: **100 GB**

    o DataDisk02: **300 GB**

    o DataDisk03: **50 GB**

    o DataDisk04: **100 GB**

    o DataDisk05: **75 GB**

2. On **CM01**, log on as **VIAMONSTRA\Administrator** using a password of **P@ssw0rd**.

3. Using **Server Manager**, **Disk Manager**, or **PowerShell**, create the following five volumes on **CM01**:

    o DataDisk01, 100 GB, (E:): **Program Files**

    o DataDisk02, 300 GB, (F:): **Content Library**

    o DataDisk03, 50 GB, (G:): **SQL TempDB**

    o DataDisk04, 100 GB, (H:): **SQL DB**

    o DataDisk05, 75 GB, (I:): **SQL Logs**

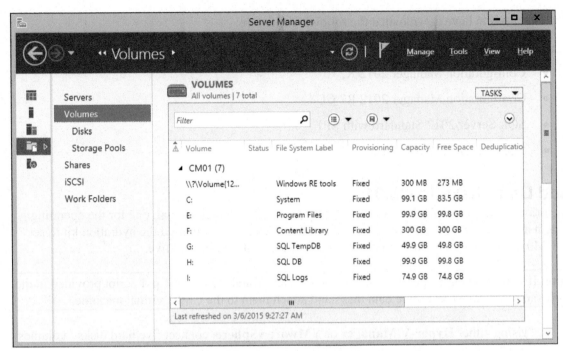

Using Server Manager to create the volumes.

Install SQL Server 2012 Standard SP1

In these steps, I assume you have downloaded the following software to CM01:

- **SQL Server 2012 Standard with SP1.** Copied to **C:\Setup\SQL2012**.

- **SQL Server 2012 SP1 CU8.** Copied to **C:\Setup\SQL2012CU**.

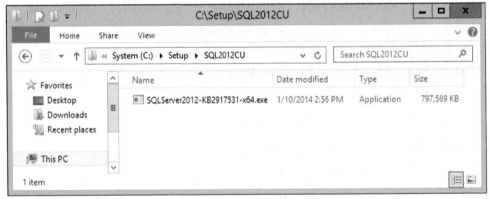

The CU8 update, requested as a hotfix and extracted to the C:\Setup\SQL2012CU folder.

Complete the following steps to install SQL Server 2012 Standard SP1 with CU8:

1. On **CM01**, log on as **VIAMONSTRA\Administrator**.

2. Copy the book sample files to **C:\Setup** on **CM01**.

3. Open an elevated **PowerShell** prompt, and install SQL Server by running the following command (the command is wrapped and should be one line):

    ```
    C:\Setup\SQL2012\setup.exe
    /Configurationfile=C:\Setup\Scripts\SQL2012Unattend.ini
    ```

Installing SQL Server 2012 Standard with SP1 and CU8.

4. When the SQL Server 2012 setup is complete, review the **Summary.txt** setup log file found in the **C:\Program Files\Microsoft SQL Server\110\Setup Bootstrap\Log** folder.

5. Exit the elevated **PowerShell** prompt.

Configure SQL Server Memory

In the minimum supported configuration, having only 16 GB of RAM on the CM01 virtual machine, you should configure SQL Server memory between 8 GB and 12 GB.

Perform the following steps to configure SQL Server memory:

1. On **CM01**, log on as **VIAMONSTRA\Administrator** using a password of **P@ssw0rd**.

2. Open an elevated **PowerShell** prompt, and configure SQL Server memory by running the following command (the command is wrapped and should be one line):

    ```
    Invoke-Sqlcmd -InputFile
    C:\Setup\Scripts\SetSQLServerMemory.sql
    ```

> **Note:** If you just installed SQL Server 2012 and are using the same PowerShell prompt as you used to run the setup, you need to exit it and open it again (elevated) for the SQL PowerShell cmdlets to be available.

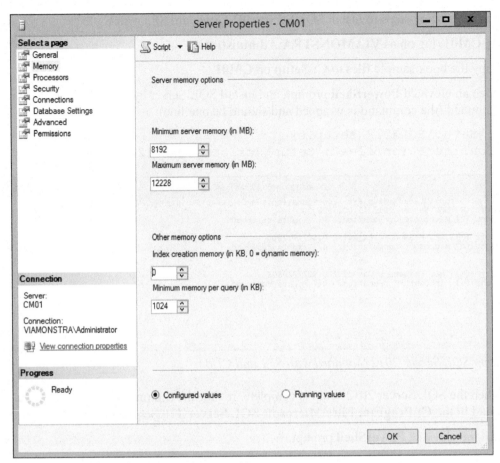

SQL Server memory configured on CM01.

Configure SQL Database Files

Before installing Configuration Manager 2012 R2, you should precreate the SQL database files for Configuration Manager, as well as configure additional database files for the TempDB. In the ViaMonstra environment with 6500 users/machines, the estimated Configuration Manager database size is 40 GB, and the CM01 virtual machines are configured with four virtual processors (equal to using four database files, per Microsoft best practices).

Perform the following steps to configure SQL database files:

1. On **CM01**, log on as **VIAMONSTRA\Administrator**.

2. Open an elevated **PowerShell** prompt, and create the four SQL database files for Configuration Manager by running the following command (the command is wrapped and should be one line):

```
Invoke-Sqlcmd -QueryTimeout 0
-InputFile C:\Setup\Scripts\CreateConfigMgrDatabase.sql
```

Note: Setting QueryTimeout to 0 means no timeout. The default timeout (30 seconds) is often not enough to create the databases, especially if the disk subsystem is slow.

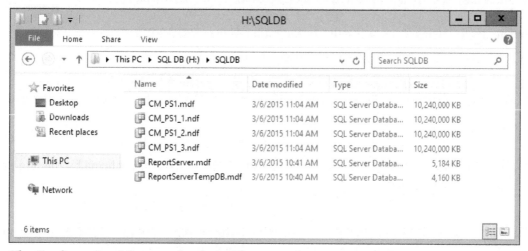

The Configuration Manager database files created.

3. In the elevated **PowerShell** prompt, create the additional SQL TempDB database files and set their initial size to a total of 16 GB by running the following command (the command is wrapped and should be one line):

```
Invoke-Sqlcmd -QueryTimeout 0
-InputFile C:\Setup\Scripts\ConfigureTempDB.sql
```

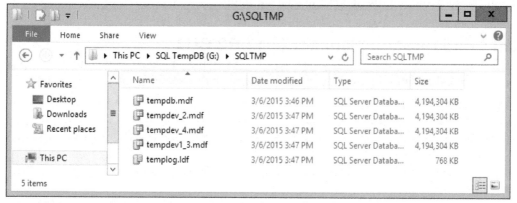

The SQL TempDB database files.

Install Configuration Manager 2012 R2

In this guide I assume you have downloaded the following to CM01:

- **Configuration Manager 2012 R2.** Copied to **C:\Setup\CM2012**.

- **Configuration Manager 2012 R2 prerequisites.** Copied to **C:\Setup\CM2012DL**.

11

> **Note:** To download the Configuration Manager 2012 R2 prerequisites, run the SMSSETUP\BIN\X64\Setupdl.exe application from the Configuration Manager 2012 R2 installation files, specify a temporary download folder, and click Download.

Complete the following steps to install Configuration Manager 2012 R2:

1. On **CM01**, log on as **VIAMONSTRA\Administrator**.

2. Open an elevated **PowerShell** prompt, create the **System Management** container in **Active Directory**, and grant permissions to the **CM01** server by running the following command:

   ```
   cscript C:\Setup\Scripts\CreateSystemManagementContainer.vbs
   ```

3. In the elevated **PowerShell** prompt, extend the **Active Directory** schema by running the following command:

   ```
   C:\Setup\CM2012\SMSSETUP\BIN\X64\extadsch.exe
   ```

4. In the elevated **PowerShell** prompt, install **Configuration Manager 2012 R2** by running the following command (the command is wrapped and should be one line):

   ```
   C:\Setup\CM2012\SMSSETUP\BIN\X64\setup.exe /Script
   C:\Setup\Scripts\CM2012Unattend.ini /NoUserInput
   ```

5. When setup is completed (watch the setup.exe and setupwpf.exe processes), review the **C:\ConfigMgrSetup.log** file.

> **Note:** You also can start CMTrace.exe from C:\Setup\CM2012\SMSSETUP\TOOLS and review the C:\ConfigMgrSetup.log file in real-time during setup.

Install Configuration Manager 2012 R2 CU4

Since the release of Configuration Manager 2012 R2, there have been several cumulative updates that include critical updates for Configuration Manager. In this section, you install CU4 for Configuration Manager 2012 R2.

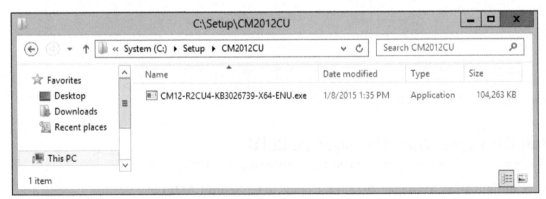

The R2 CU4 update (KB3026739) downloaded to C:\Setup\CM2012CU on CM01.

In these steps, I assume you have downloaded the KB3026739 update to C:\Setup\CM2012CU on CM01.

1. On **CM01**, open an elevated **PowerShell** prompt, and verify that are no pending reboots by running the following command:

```
C:\Setup\Scripts\Test-PendingReboot.ps1
```

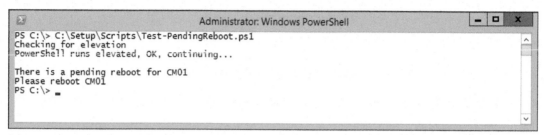

The Test-PendingReboot.ps1 script detecting a pending reboot.

2. If there is a pending reboot, run the **Restart-Computer** command to restart **CM01**. After the reboot, log in again, and open an elevated **PowerShell** prompt.

3. Make sure the **Configuration Manager console** is closed before continuing.

4. Install **Configuration Manager 2012 R2 CU4** by running the following command (the command is wrapped and should be one line):

```
C:\Setup\CM2012CU\CM12-R2CU4-KB3026739-X64-ENU.exe
/Unattended
```

5. When the setup is completed, check the **cm12-r2cu4-kb3026739-x64-enu.log** and **ConfigMgrUpdateSetup.log** files in the **C:\Windows\Temp** folder.

Real World Note: If you see the CU4 update stop on "Stopping service WINMGMT", open Services and stop the Windows Management Instrumentation service manually. The update will then continue.

6. Verify the CU Level installed by running this command (the command is wrapped and should be one line):

```
Get-ItemProperty -Path HKLM:\SOFTWARE\Microsoft\SMS\Setup
-Name "CULevel"
```

7. Exit the **PowerShell** prompt, and start the **Configuration Manager console** once to configure the PowerShell module (needed for the script in the next step to work).

8. Open an elevated **PowerShell** prompt again, and create the additional four CU4 update packages for secondary site servers, consoles, and x86/x64 clients by running the following command:

```
C:\Setup\Scripts\Create-CU4UpdatePackages.ps1
```

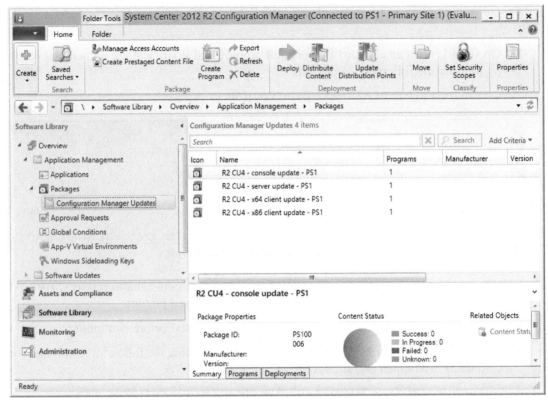

The Configuration Manager console, showing the CU4 packages.

Configure Discovery Methods

Discovery methods enable the Configuration Manager site to query Active Directory to locate IP subnets, Active Directory sites, and system information. This information is used to create boundary groups in the next section.

1.   On **CM01**, log on as **VIAMONSTRA\Administrator**.

2.   Open an elevated **PowerShell** prompt, and configure **Active Directory Forest Discovery** by running the following command:

    ```
    C:\Setup\Scripts\EnableADForestDiscovery.ps1
    ```

3.   In the elevated **PowerShell** prompt, verify that the boundaries are created as part of enabling Active Directory System Discovery by running the following command (it may take a little while for the boundaries to be created):

    ```
    Get-CMBoundary
    ```

4.   In the elevated **PowerShell** prompt, configure **Active Directory System Discovery** by running the following command:

    ```
    C:\Setup\Scripts\EnableADSystemDiscovery.ps1
    ```

Create a Boundary Group

To make sure clients can locate content on the distribution point and find the management point, you configure a boundary group.

1. On **CM01**, log on as **VIAMONSTRA\Administrator**.

2. Open an elevated **PowerShell** prompt, and create a boundary group by running the following command:

    ```
    C:\Setup\Scripts\CreateBoundaryGroup.ps1
    ```

Install the Clients Using a Startup Script

In this guide you use a computer startup script to install the Configuration Manager client on CM01 and PC0001–PC0004. Jason Sandys, the creator of the script, kindly allowed me to include his script in the book sample files. For more information, check out this link: http://blog.configmgrftw.com/?page_id=349.

In these steps, I assume that you have downloaded the startup script, which is available as part of the book sample files, and copied it to C:\Setup\ConfigMgrStartup on CM01.

1. On **CM01**, log on as **VIAMONSTRA\Administrator**.

2. Open an elevated **PowerShell** prompt, and create a **Configuration Manager** package source folder structure by running the following command:

    ```
    C:\Setup\Scripts\Create-ConfigMgrFolders.ps1
    ```

3. Using **File Explorer**, navigate to the **E:\Program Files\Microsoft Configuration Manager\Client** folder.

    Copy the **ccmsetup.exe** file to the previously created **F:\Sources\Software\CMClient\Install** folder (created by the script).

4. Using **File Explorer**, navigate to the **E:\Program Files\Microsoft Configuration Manager\hotfix\KB3026739\Client** folder.

    Copy the **i386** and **x64** folders to **F:\Sources\Software\CMClient\Hotfixes**.

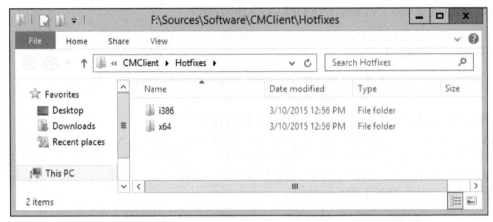

The F:\Sources\Software\CMClient\Hotfixes folder with hotfixes added.

5. On **DC01**, log on as **VIAMONSTRA\Administrator**, open the **Group Policy Management console**, and complete the following:

    a. Expand **Forest: corp.viamonstra.com / Domains / corp.viamonstra.com / ViaMonstra**.

    b. Right-click **Group Policy Objects** and select **New**.

    c. Name the new group policy **Install ConfigMgr 2012 Client Agent** and click **OK**.

    d. Expand **Group Policy Objects**, right-click the **Install ConfigMgr 2012 Client Agent** GPO, and select **Edit**.

    e. Select **Computer Configuration / Policies / Windows Settings / Scripts (Startup/Shutdown)**.

    f. Right-click **Startup** and select **Properties**.

    g. Click **Add**, and click **Browse**; then copy **ConfigMgrStartup.vbs** and **ConfigMgrStartup.xml** from **\\CM01\C$\Setup\ConfigMgrStartup** to the folder that was opened when you clicked **Browse**. Then select the **ConfigMgrStartup.vbs** file.

    h. In **Script Parameters**, type **/Config:ConfigMgrStartup.xml** and click **OK** twice. Then close the **Group Policy Management Editor**.

The Startup properties.

6. Expand **ViaMonstra**, right-click the **Servers** OU and select **Link an Existing GPO**.

7. From the **Group Policy Objects**, select **Install ConfigMgr 2012 Client Agent**, and click **OK**.

8. Restart **CM01** to apply the new computer-based GPO. After restarting, you can verify the client installation process by reviewing the **ConfigMgrStartup.vbs.log** file in the **C:\Windows\Temp** folder on **CM01**.

9. On **DC01**, right-click the **Workstations** OU and select **Link an Existing GPO**.

10. From the **Group Policy Objects**, select **Install ConfigMgr 2012 Client Agent**, and click **OK**.

11. Start or restart **PC0001–PC0004** to apply the new computer-based GPO. After restarting, you can verify the client installation process by reviewing the **ConfigMgrStartup.vbs.log** file in the **C:\Windows\Temp** folder.

Real World Note: If the policy doesn't apply, run gpupdate /force on the clients and do another restart. Sometimes group policy software installation needs some "encouragement" to run.

17

Enable Firewall for SQL Server 2012

Similar to a production environment, queries and report creation are usually done from a client. By default, Windows Server 2012 is more secure than previous versions of Windows Server. In this section, you enable the appropriate Windows Server 2012 firewall rules to allow access to SQL Server. This step allows our development client to communicate with SQL Server.

In these steps, I assume you have downloaded the book sample files to the C:\Setup on CM01.

1. On **CM01**, open an elevated **PowerShell** prompt, and to open the firewall rules for SQL Server, execute the following script:

```
C:\Setup\Scripts\EnableSQLServerFirewall.ps1
```

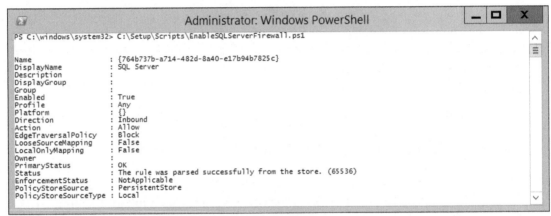

The EnableSQLFirewall.ps1 script updating the firewall rules.

Chapter 2

Reporting Services Installation

In this chapter, you learn about enabling the Configuration Manager 2012 Reporting Services Role and troubleshooting SQL Server Reporting Service.

Step-by-Step Guide Requirements

If you want to follow the step-by-step guides in this chapter, you need a lab environment configured as outlined in Chapter 1 and Appendix A. In this chapter, you use the following virtual machines:

DC01

CM01

The VMs used in this chapter.

No additional software is needed for this chapter.

Reporting Services Installation Location

As part of the lab environment, Configuration Manager 2012 is installed on the same server as SQL Server. SQL Server Reporting Services (SSRS) was installed with the initial, automated SQL Server setup. The next step is configuring the Configuration Manager 2012 reporting services role.

In this scenario, SSRS is installed on the same server running SQL Server. This is the recommended configuration and optimal for most Configuration Manager environments.

The major advantages/benefits of SSRS installed on the same server as SQL Server follow:

- Less complex

- Easier to implement

- Fewer setup, connection, and communication issues

    SQL SPN (Service Principle Names) missing or invalid

- Invalid or missing firewall rules/ports

- Fewer authentication issues

- Higher performance

    Network connection is not relevant for SSRS communication with SQL Server.

> **Note:** If SSRS needs to be installed on a remote server, refer to the following blog post to install and configure: http://www.scconfigmgr.com/2015/02/25/install-and-configure-a-remote-reporting-services-point-in-configmgr-2012/.

Enabling the Reporting Services Role

In this section, you enable Configuration Manager 2012 to use SQL Server Reporting Services:

1. On **CM01**, log on as **VIAMONSTA\Administrator**. If you are using the lab environment built from the hydration kit, the password is **P@ssw0rd**.

2. Launch the **Configuration Manager console**.

3. Open the **Administration** workspace.

4. Expand **Site Configuration**, and then select **Servers and Site System Roles**.

5. Right-click the server **CM01.corp.viamonstra.com**, and then select **Add Site System Roles**.

    You should see the following **Add Site Systems Roles Wizard** :

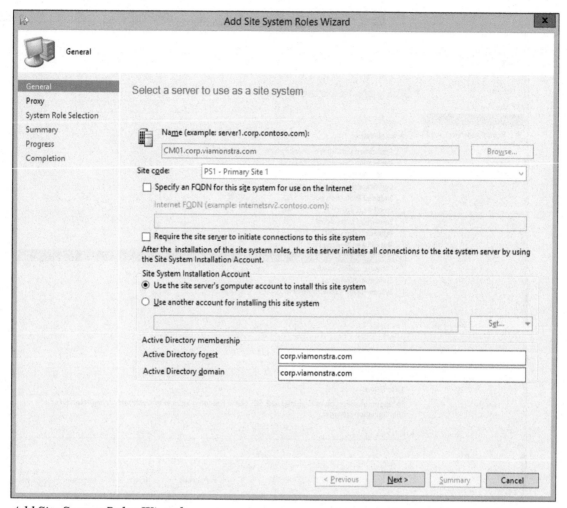

Add Site System Roles Wizard.

6. On the **General** page, click **Next**.

7. On the **Proxy** page, click **Next**.

8. On the **System Role Selection** page, in the **Available roles** list, select **Reporting services point**, and click **Next**.

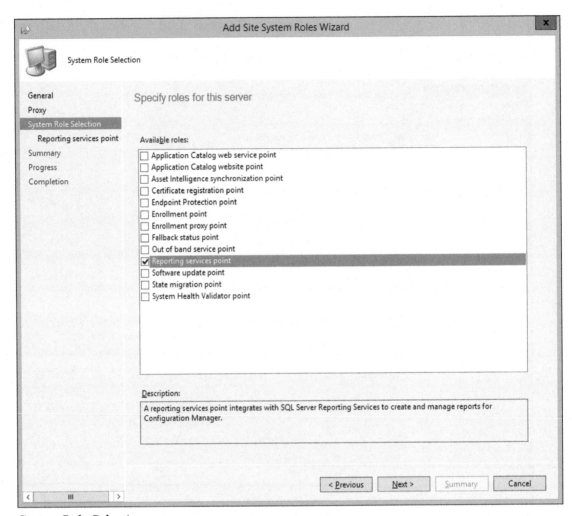

System Role Selection.

9. On the **Specify Reporting Services settings** page, take the following actions:

   a. Click **Verify** to verify the site server and database connection.

   b. At the **Specify the credentials** section, click **Set** and **New Account**. Then click **Browse** to locate and select the **CM_SR** account in the **VIAMONSTRA** domain. Enter the password **(P@ssw0rd)** in both locations, click **OK**, and then click **Next**.

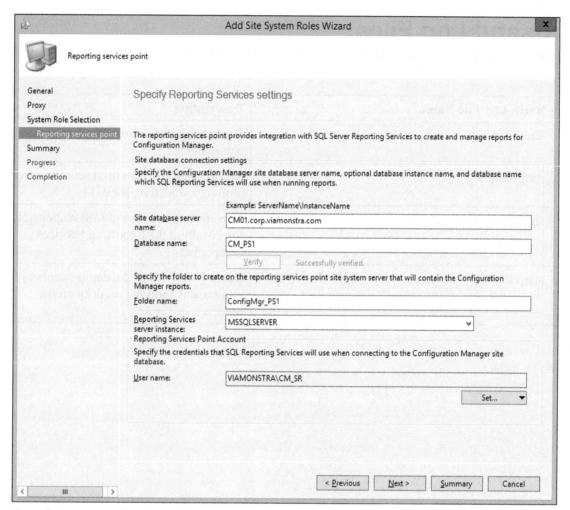

Specify Reporting Services settings.

10. You are presented with the Summary page. Click **Next**.

11. The **Completion** page should indicate successful completion. Click **Close**.

Useful Log Files

The following Configuration Manager log files can be helpful to monitor the installation activity and in troubleshooting failed installs.

SSRS Log File Name	Description
sitecomp.log	Records maintenance of the installed site components
srsrpsetup.log	Records activity for initial setup activity, monitors launching the MSI
srsrpMSI.log	Records activity for the MSI responsible for installing the Reporting Services component
srsrp.log	Records activity of the deployments of the reports and applying security on the reports

Chapter 3

Information Data Mining

All reports rely on queries to retrieve data from one or more databases. One of the more challenging exercises in Configuration Manager 2012 is finding the data you need to create the report. In this chapter, you explore several different techniques for locating the data you need.

Advanced query topics are beyond the scope of this book.

Step-by-Step Guide Requirements

If you want to follow the step-by-step guides in this chapter, you need a lab environment configured as outlined in Chapter 1 and to have configured Reporting Services in Chapter 2 and Appendix A. In this chapter, you use the following virtual machines:

DC01   CM01   PC0001

The VMs used in this chapter.

You also need to have downloaded the following software:

- SQL Server 2012 SP1
- SQL Server 2012 SP1 CU8

Install SQL Server 2012 SP1 Tools on PC0001

In these steps, I assume you have downloaded the following software to PC0001.

- **SQL Server 2012 with SP1.** Copied to **C:\Setup\SQL2012**.
- **SQL Server 2012 SP1 CU8.** Copied to **C:\Setup\SQL2012CU**.
- **Book sample files.** Copied to **C:\Setup**.

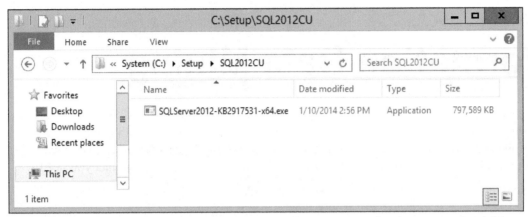

The CU8 update, requested as a hotfix and extracted to the C:\Setup\SQL2012CU folder.

Complete the following steps to install SQL Server 2012 SP1 with CU8:

1. On **PC0001**, log on as **VIAMONSTRA\Administrator**.

2. Open an elevated **PowerShell** prompt, and install **SQL Server** by running the following command (the command is wrapped and should be one line):

```
C:\Setup\SQL2012\setup.exe
/Configurationfile=C:\Setup\Scripts\SQL2012ToolsUnattend.ini
```

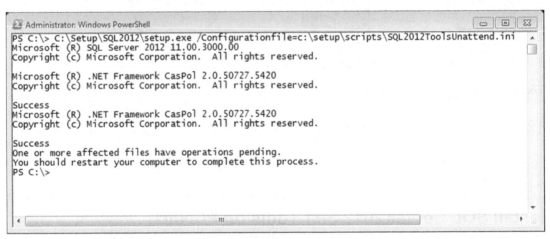

Installing SQL Server 2012 SP1 Tools on PC0001.

3. When the SQL Server 2012 SP1 setup is complete, review the **Summary.txt** setup log file found in the **C:\Program Files\Microsoft SQL Server\110\Setup Bootstrap\Log** folder.

4. Restart **PC0001** by running the following command:

```
Restart-Computer
```

Views

Think of a SQL Server view as a virtual table that derives its data from an underlying query. Views often mask the underlying complexity of the underlying query or queries.

Configuration Manager 2012 (and previous versions) make extensive use of views. There are two types of views created within the product:

- **Static views.** Created at time of product install

- **Dynamic views.** Automatically created from new tables that are created (i.e. new collections)

Advantages of using views:

- Views simplify the underlying complexity of tables.

- Columns can be renamed.

- View consistency is maintained from Configuration Manager updates from version to version.

- No really advanced SQL knowledge is needed in order to use a view.

Real World Note: While it possible to create queries using the Configuration Manager tables, it is considered a best practice to use views to create your report queries. Microsoft has promised view compatibility from version to version. Service pack updates may make changes to tables, which in turn may cause your queries to no longer function!

View Categories

Here are the categories for Configuration Manager 2012 views, the first three of which relate to information found in Active Directory and client inventory:

- **Discovery.** Views that can be used to report on data discovered within Active Directory by Configuration Manager 2012 and start with a "v_R_*" prefix

- **Inventory.** Views used to report on inventory data (hardware, software, and so on) that is passed back to Configuration Manager 2012 as a result of the Configuration Manager 2012 agent. These views start with a "v_GS_*" prefix. Generally, the latest record from the most recent inventory is stored in the underlying tables.

- **History.** Views used to report on historical inventory data. These views start with a "v_HS_*" prefix. As fresh data can be found in the Inventory tables, the older data can be found in the History views. For example, these historical views can be used for purposes such as triggering an alert if the total memory on a device is suddenly reduced.

- **Other views.** There are a number of other supporting views that provide information about the Configuration Manager site, such as collections, site systems, packages, and applications. Additionally, other examples include information about compliance, security updates, deployments, and anti-virus related activity.

Available Views

This section is meant to provide a list of available views for client-specific information. The next section provides more information on how to locate the views you need.

Discovery Views

Discovery information is the core tenant of many queries. Discovery is primarily derived from Active Directory, with one exception. The view v_R_System_Valid qualifies the information returned from the view as Not Obsolete, Not Decommission and an Active client. As such, v_R_System_Valid is a good view to use at the core of many reports to help prevent queries from returning outdated or incorrect information.

Discovery View Names
v_R_System
v_R_System_Valid
v_R_UnknownSystem
v_R_User
V_R_UserGroup

Inventory Views

Inventory views contain information that is derived from recent Configuration Manager client inventory. As each inventory cycle is processed, the data for the Inventory view is updated, and the older record gets moved to the Historical views.

Inventory View Names	
v_GS_1394_CONTROLLER	v_GS_ACTIVESYNC_CONNECTED_DEVICE
v_GS_ACTIVESYNC_SERVICE	v_GS_ADD_REMOVE_PROGRAMS
v_GS_ADD_REMOVE_PROGRAMS_64	v_GS_ADVANCED_CLIENT_PORTS
v_GS_ADVANCED_CLIENT_SSL_CONFIGURATIONS	v_GS_AMT_AGENT
v_GS_AntimalwareHealthStatus	v_GS_AntimalwareInfectionStatus
v_GS_APPV_CLIENT_APPLICATION	v_GS_APPV_CLIENT_PACKAGE
v_GS_AUTOSTART_SOFTWARE	v_GS_BASEBOARD
v_GS_BATTERY	v_GS_BOOT_CONFIGURATION
v_GS_BROWSER_HELPER_OBJECT	v_GS_CCM_RECENTLY_USED_APPS

Inventory View Names	
v_GS_CDROM	v_GS_CollectedFile
v_GS_COMPUTER_SYSTEM	v_GS_COMPUTER_SYSTEM_PRODUCT
v_GS_DESKTOP	v_GS_DESKTOP_MONITOR
v_GS_DEVICE_BLUETOOTH	v_GS_DEVICE_CAMERA
v_GS_DEVICE_CERTIFICATES	v_GS_DEVICE_CLIENT
v_GS_DEVICE_CLIENTAGENTVERSION	v_GS_DEVICE_COMPUTERSYSTEM
v_GS_DEVICE_DISPLAY	v_GS_DEVICE_EMAIL
v_GS_DEVICE_ENCRYPTION	v_GS_DEVICE_EXCHANGE
v_GS_DEVICE_INFO	v_GS_DEVICE_INSTALLED APPLICATIONS
v_GS_DEVICE_IRDA	v_GS_DEVICE_MEMORY
v_GS_DEVICE_MEMORY_ADDRESS	v_GS_DEVICE_OSINFORMATION
v_GS_DEVICE_PASSWORD	v_GS_DEVICE_POLICY
v_GS_DEVICE_POWER	v_GS_DEVICE_WINDOWSSECURITY POLICY
v_GS_DEVICE_WLAN	v_GS_DISK
v_GS_DMA_CHANNEL	v_GS_DRIVER_VXD
v_GS_EMBEDDED_DEVICE_INFO	v_GS_ENCRYPTABLE_VOLUME
v_GS_ENVIRONMENT	v_GS_EPDeploymentState
v_GS_FOLDER_REDIRECTION_HEALTH	v_GS_IDE_CONTROLLER
v_GS_INSTALLED_EXECUTABLE	v_GS_INSTALLED_SOFTWARE
v_GS_INSTALLED_SOFTWARE_ CATEGORIZED	v_GS_INSTALLED_SOFTWARE_MS
v_GS_IRQ	v_GS_KEYBOARD_DEVICE
v_GS_LastSoftwareScan	v_GS_LOAD_ORDER_GROUP
v_GS_LOGICAL_DISK	v_GS_Mapped_Add_Remove_Programs
v_GS_MODEM_DEVICE	v_GS_MOTHERBOARD_DEVICE
v_GS_NAPCLIENT	v_GS_NETWORK_ADAPTER
v_GS_NETWORK_ADAPTER_ CONFIGURATION	v_GS_NETWORK_CLIENT

Inventory View Names	
v_GS_NETWORK_LOGIN_PROFILE	v_GS_NT_EVENTLOG_FILE
v_GS_OPERATING_SYSTEM	v_GS_OS_RECOVERY_CONFIGURATION
v_GS_PAGE_FILE_SETTING	v_GS_PARALLEL_PORT
v_GS_PARTITION	v_GS_PC_BIOS
v_GS_PCMCIA_CONTROLLER	v_GS_PHYSICAL_MEMORY
v_GS_PNP_DEVICE_DRIVER	v_GS_POINTING_DEVICE
v_GS_PORT	v_GS_PORTABLE_BATTERY
v_GS_POWER_MANAGEMENT_CAPABILITIES	v_GS_POWER_MANAGEMENT_CLIENT_OPTOUT_SETTINGS
v_GS_POWER_MANAGEMENT_CONFIGURATION	v_GS_POWER_MANAGEMENT_DAY
v_GS_POWER_MANAGEMENT_MONTH	v_GS_POWER_MANAGEMENT_SETTINGS
v_GS_POWER_MANAGEMENT_SUSPEND_ERROR	v_GS_POWER_SUPPLY
v_GS_PRINT_JOB	v_GS_PRINTER_CONFIGURATION
v_GS_PRINTER_DEVICE	v_GS_PROCESS
v_GS_PROCESSOR	v_GS_PROTECTED_VOLUME_INFO
v_GS_PROTOCOL	v_GS_QUICK_FIX_ENGINEERING
v_GS_RAX_APPLICATION	v_GS_REGISTRY
v_GS_SCSI_CONTROLLER	v_GS_SERIAL_PORT
v_GS_SERIAL_PORT_CONFIGURATION	v_GS_SERVER_FEATURE
v_GS_SERVICE	v_GS_SHARE
v_GS_SMS_ADVANCED_CLIENT_STATE	v_GS_SOFTWARE_LICENSING_PRODUCT
v_GS_SOFTWARE_LICENSING_SERVICE	v_GS_SOFTWARE_SHORTCUT
v_GS_SOFTWARE_TAG	v_GS_SoftwareFile
v_GS_SoftwareProduct	v_GS_SoftwareUsageData
v_GS_SOUND_DEVICE	v_GS_SYSTEM
v_GS_SYSTEM_ACCOUNT	v_GS_SYSTEM_CONSOLE_USAGE

Inventory View Names	
v_GS_SYSTEM_CONSOLE_USAGE_MAX GROUP	v_GS_SYSTEM_CONSOLE_USER
v_GS_SYSTEM_DEVICES	v_GS_SYSTEM_DRIVER
v_GS_SYSTEM_ENCLOSURE	v_GS_SYSTEM_ENCLOSURE_UNIQUE
v_GS_SYSTEMHEALTHAGENT	v_GS_TAPE_DRIVE
v_GS_Threats	v_GS_TIME_ZONE
v_GS_TPM	v_GS_TS_ISSUED_LICENSE
v_GS_TS_LICENSE_KEY_PACK	v_GS_UnknownFile
v_GS_USB_CONTROLLER	v_GS_USB_DEVICE
v_GS_USER_PROFILE	v_GS_VIDEO_CONTROLLER
v_GS_VIRTUAL_APPLICATION_PACKAGES	v_GS_VIRTUAL_APPLICATIONS
v_GS_VIRTUAL_MACHINE	v_GS_VIRTUAL_MACHINE_64
v_GS_VIRTUAL_MACHINE_EXT	v_GS_WEBAPP_APPLICATION
v_GS_WINDOWS8_APPLICATION	v_GS_WINDOWS8_APPLICATION_USER_INFO
v_GS_WINDOWSUPDATEAGENT VERSION	v_GS_WORKSTATION_STATUS
v_GS_WRITE_FILTER_STATE	v_GS_X86_PC_MEMORY

History Views

The History views contain information previously stored in the Inventory views. These views tend not to be used as much as the Inventory views, but can be useful to detect changes in client information between inventory cycles.

History View Names	
v_HS_1394_CONTROLLER	v_HS_ACTIVESYNC_CONNECTED_DEVICE
v_HS_ACTIVESYNC_SERVICE	v_HS_ADD_REMOVE_PROGRAMS
v_HS_ADD_REMOVE_PROGRAMS_64	v_HS_ADVANCED_CLIENT_PORTS
v_HS_ADVANCED_CLIENT_SSL_CONFIGURATIONS	v_HS_AMT_AGENT

History View Names	
v_HS_APPV_CLIENT_APPLICATION	v_HS_APPV_CLIENT_PACKAGE
v_HS_AUTOSTART_SOFTWARE	v_HS_BASEBOARD
v_HS_BATTERY	v_HS_BOOT_CONFIGURATION
v_HS_BROWSER_HELPER_OBJECT	v_HS_CDROM
v_HS_COMPUTER_SYSTEM	v_HS_COMPUTER_SYSTEM_PRODUCT
v_HS_DESKTOP	v_HS_DESKTOP_MONITOR
v_HS_DEVICE_BLUETOOTH	v_HS_DEVICE_CAMERA
v_HS_DEVICE_CERTIFICATES	v_HS_DEVICE_CLIENT
v_HS_DEVICE_CLIENTAGENT VERSION	v_HS_DEVICE_COMPUTERSYSTEM
v_HS_DEVICE_DISPLAY	v_HS_DEVICE_EMAIL
v_HS_DEVICE_ENCRYPTION	v_HS_DEVICE_EXCHANGE
v_HS_DEVICE_INSTALLED APPLICATIONS	v_HS_DEVICE_IRDA
v_HS_DEVICE_MEMORY	v_HS_DEVICE_MEMORY_ADDRESS
v_HS_DEVICE_OSINFORMATION	v_HS_DEVICE_PASSWORD
v_HS_DEVICE_POLICY	v_HS_DEVICE_POWER
v_HS_DEVICE_WINDOWSSECURITY POLICY	v_HS_DEVICE_WLAN
v_HS_DISK	v_HS_DMA_CHANNEL
v_HS_DRIVER_VXD	v_HS_EMBEDDED_DEVICE_INFO
v_HS_ENCRYPTABLE_VOLUME	v_HS_ENVIRONMENT
v_HS_IDE_CONTROLLER	v_HS_INSTALLED_EXECUTABLE
v_HS_INSTALLED_SOFTWARE	v_HS_IRQ
v_HS_KEYBOARD_DEVICE	v_HS_LOAD_ORDER_GROUP
v_HS_LOGICAL_DISK	v_HS_MODEM_DEVICE
v_HS_MOTHERBOARD_DEVICE	v_HS_NAPCLIENT
v_HS_NETWORK_ADAPTER	v_HS_NETWORK_ADAPTER_ CONFIGURATION
v_HS_NETWORK_CLIENT	v_HS_NETWORK_LOGIN_PROFILE

History View Names	
v_HS_NT_EVENTLOG_FILE	v_HS_OPERATING_SYSTEM
v_HS_OS_RECOVERY_CONFIGURATION	v_HS_PAGE_FILE_SETTING
v_HS_PARALLEL_PORT	v_HS_PARTITION
v_HS_PC_BIOS	v_HS_PCMCIA_CONTROLLER
v_HS_PHYSICAL_MEMORY	v_HS_POINTING_DEVICE
v_HS_PORT	v_HS_PORTABLE_BATTERY
v_HS_POWER_SUPPLY	v_HS_PRINT_JOB
v_HS_PRINTER_CONFIGURATION	v_HS_PRINTER_DEVICE
v_HS_PROCESS	v_HS_PROCESSOR
v_HS_PROTECTED_VOLUME_INFO	v_HS_PROTOCOL
v_HS_QUICK_FIX_ENGINEERING	v_HS_RAX_APPLICATION
v_HS_REGISTRY	v_HS_SCSI_CONTROLLER
v_HS_SERIAL_PORT	v_HS_SERIAL_PORT_CONFIGURATION
v_HS_SERVER_FEATURE	v_HS_SERVICE
v_HS_SHARE	v_HS_SMS_ADVANCED_CLIENT_STATE
v_HS_SOFTWARE_LICENSING_PRODUCT	v_HS_SOFTWARE_LICENSING_SERVICE
v_HS_SOFTWARE_SHORTCUT	v_HS_SOFTWARE_TAG
v_HS_SOUND_DEVICE	v_HS_SYSTEM
v_HS_SYSTEM_ACCOUNT	v_HS_SYSTEM_CONSOLE_USAGE
v_HS_SYSTEM_CONSOLE_USER	v_HS_SYSTEM_DRIVER
v_HS_SYSTEM_ENCLOSURE	v_HS_SYSTEMHEALTHAGENT
v_HS_TAPE_DRIVE	v_HS_TIME_ZONE
v_HS_TPM	v_HS_TS_ISSUED_LICENSE
v_HS_TS_LICENSE_KEY_PACK	v_HS_USB_CONTROLLER
v_HS_USB_DEVICE	v_HS_VIDEO_CONTROLLER
v_HS_VIRTUAL_APPLICATION_PACKAGES	v_HS_VIRTUAL_APPLICATIONS
v_HS_VIRTUAL_MACHINE	v_HS_VIRTUAL_MACHINE_64

History View Names	
v_HS_VIRTUAL_MACHINE_EXT	v_HS_WEBAPP_APPLICATION
v_HS_WINDOWS8_APPLICATION	v_HS_WINDOWS8_APPLICATION_USER _INFO
v_HS_WINDOWSUPDATEAGENT VERSION	v_HS_WRITE_FILTER_STATE
v_HS_X86_PC_MEMORY	

How to Locate Views (How to Find What You Need)

In this section you review several techniques to locate the information you need. I suggest that you download the reference information contained in the "Resources" section of this chapter.

Note: At time of installation, over 1,440 views are created for Configuration Manager!

In the following scenario, you need to locate the available views to identify the operating system. Complete the following steps to learn how to filter for relevant view names:

1. On **PC0001**, log on as **VIAMONSTRA\Administrator**.

2. Start and run the **SQL Server Management Studio** (SSMS) console.

3. When prompted for a connection, enter **CM01** for **Server name** and connect using **Windows Authentication**. Click **Connect**.

The Connect to Server dialog box.

4. In the **SSMS console**, in the left pane, expand the **Databases** node, expand the **CM_PS1** node (the Configuration Manager database), and then expand the **Views** node.

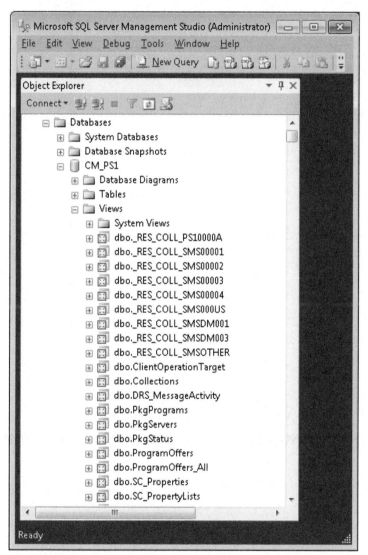

List of Configuration Manager views.

5. To filter the views displayed, click **Views** and then click the **Filter** button (the funnel) on the toolbar.

6. In the **Filter Settings** dialog box, in the **Name** row, enter **Operating** in the **Value** column.

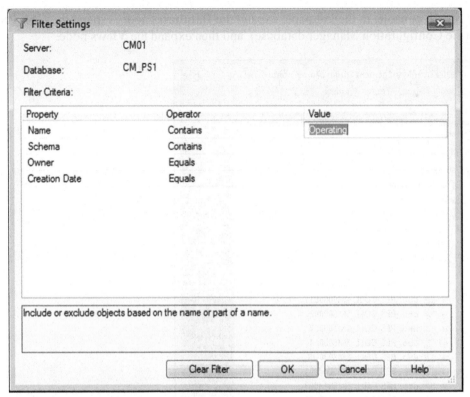

Filter Settings dialog box.

7. Click **OK**.

   You should see a filtered list of only views with "Operating" in their name.

8. Select view **dbo.v_GS_OPERATING_SYSTEM**, right-click, and choose **Select TOP 1000 Rows**.

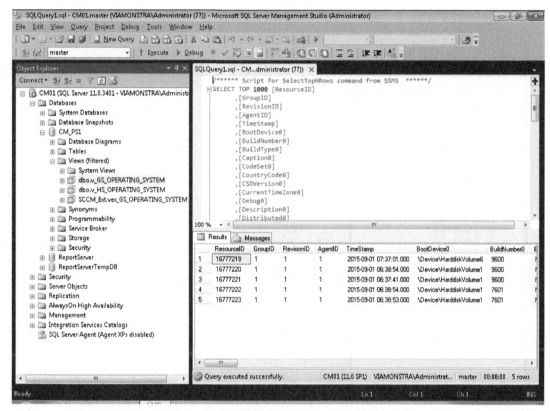

Select TOP 1000 results from v_GS_OPERATING_SYSTEM.

Note: Observe the Results tab. Scroll to the right to view other column information. Here, you are looking for fields of interest to build queries for our reports!

9. Navigate to the **SQLQuery1.sql** SQL query, locate the **SELECT TOP 1000**, and change the **1000** value to **3**. Click the **Execute** button to rerun the query, and note that there are now three rows displayed in the Results tab.

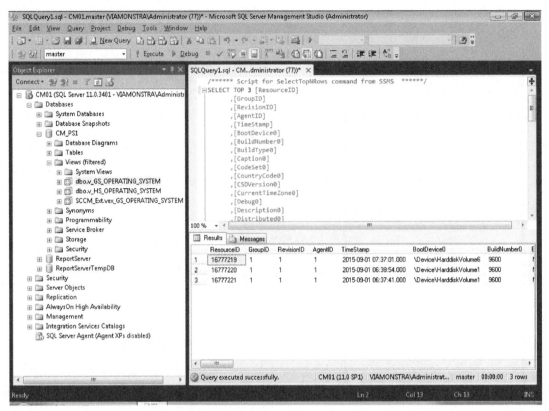

Data filtering by using custom TOP n clause.

> **Note**: This technique is a form of data sampling and a handy way to restrict the amount of data returned by the result set, especially from large databases.

Key Concept

Note the first column in the result set is the ResourceID, this is a *primary key* field (unique identifier) for each row returned from the view. You'll find that client-related views contain either ResourceID or MachineID as the primary key field. In query creation for reports, it is usually necessary to join views to combine results. This joining occurs using the primary key.

Putting It All Together

In this scenario, you need to create a query using the v_GS_OPERATING_SYSTEM view to retrieve the operating system, service pack, last boot-up time, and the NETBIOS name for the operating system. Getting the NETBIOS name requires a join to the v_R_System_Valid view.

If you are skilled in creating queries, you can write your query using native T-SQL (Transact SQL) in the New Query interface. However, an excellent way to design and interactively build your query is to use the Query Designer utility. This technique is demonstrated next.

1. Using the **SSMS console** opened in the last task, in the database drop-down list, select **CM_PS1**.

2. On the toolbar, click the **New Query** button to start a new query.

3. From the menu bar, select **Query / Design Query in Editor** (shortcut keys: Ctrl + Shift + Q).

4. Select the **Views** tab. Then locate and select **v_GS_OPERATING_SYSTEM** and click **Add**.

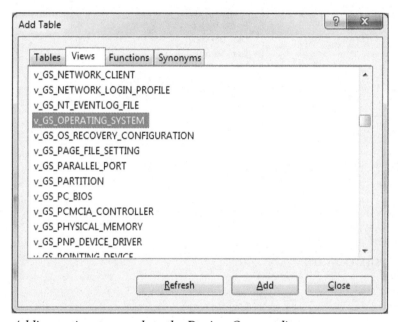

Adding a view to populate the Design Query editor.

5. In the **Add Table** dialog box, in the **Views** tab, locate and select **v_R_System_Valid**, click **Add**, and then click **Close**. You should now see both views in the Query Designer window.

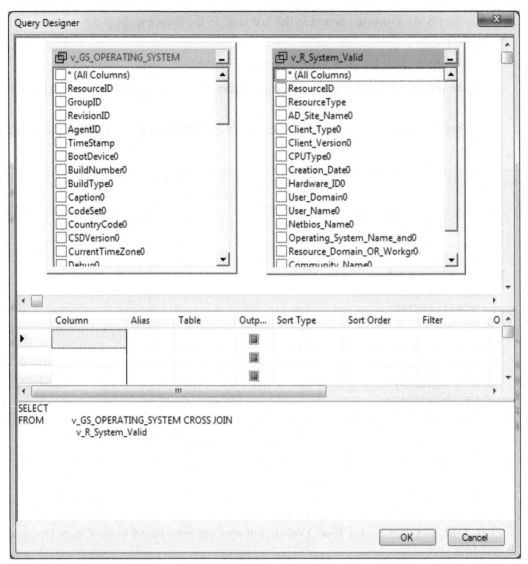

The Query Designer interface prior to joining views.

6. Now, you need to join the views. Under the **v_R_System_Valid** view, drag and drop the **ResourceID** to the corresponding **ResourceID** column in the **v_GS_OPERATING_SYSTEM** view. You should now see the two views linked in the Query Designer window.

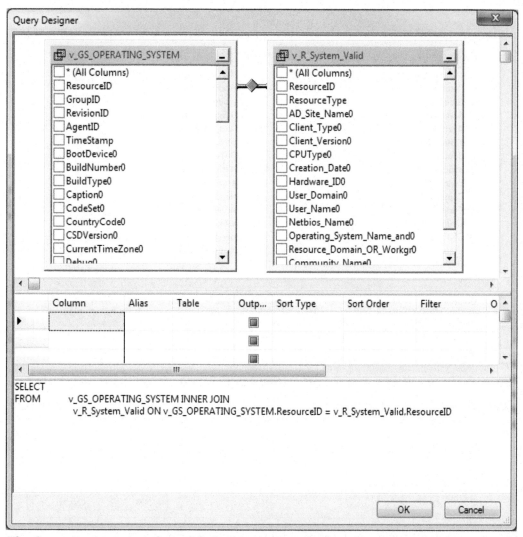

The Query Designer interface with the views now joined.

7. Now that the views have been joined, from the **v_R_System_Valid** view, select the check box for **NetbiosName0**. From the **v_GS_OPERATING_SYSTEM** view, select the check box for **Caption0**, **CSDVersion0**, and **LastBootUPTime0**.

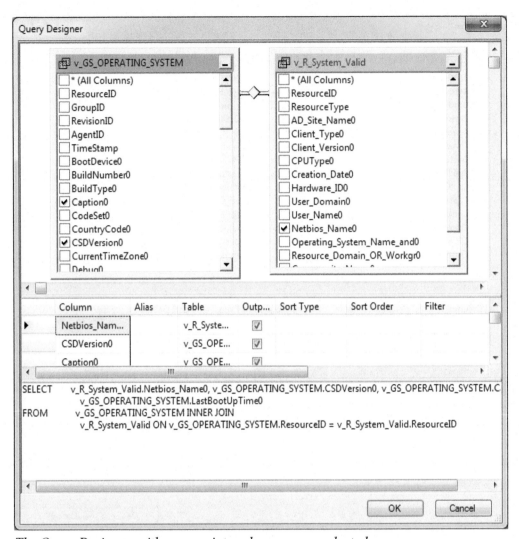

The Query Designer, with appropriate column names selected.

8. Click **OK**, and the SQL query is copied into the query window. The query should appear as follows:

```
SELECT _R_System_Valid.Netbios_Name0,
v_GS_OPERATING_SYSTEM.CSDVersion0,
v_GS_OPERATING_SYSTEM.Caption0,
v_GS_OPERATING_SYSTEM.LastBootUpTime0

FROM v_GS_OPERATING_SYSTEM

INNER JOIN v_R_System_Valid ON
v_GS_OPERATING_SYSTEM.ResourceID =
v_R_System_Valid.ResourceID
```

9. Click the **Execute** button (shortcut keys: CTRL + E) to view the results.

> **Note**: If additional modifications are required, select the SQL generated in the last step, start the Query Designer utility, and modify the query as needed. It is quite common to spend time modifying the query during this phase. Spending time on this portion can save significant time later!

10. When satisfied with the query and ready to save it, click **File / Save SQLQuery2 As**. In the **Save File As** dialog box, for **File name**, type **OSInformation** and then click **Save**. The query is saved with a *.sql file type.

Using View Column Name Aliases

While not essential to creating a view, it is often worth taking the extra step to create an alias for each of your column names. This involves adding the AS clause after each column name with a column alias and an alias abbreviation after the view names located after the query's FROM clause. Copy the following query into the SSMS query window, execute it, and observe the results.

```
SELECT vs.Netbios_Name0 AS NetbiosName,

 vOS.CSDVersion0 AS ServicePack,

 vOS.Caption0 AS OperatingSystem,

 vOS.LastBootUpTime0 AS LastBootUpTime

FROM  v_GS_OPERATING_SYSTEM vOS

INNER JOIN v_R_System_Valid vs ON vOS.ResourceID = vs.ResourceID
```

> **Note**: This query is functionally equivalent to the query in step 8 in the preceding section and easier to read. The column names require little or no change when used in reports. These aliases are used for the remainder of the book.

Resources

The following resources are useful articles from Microsoft and other community sources as appropriate:

Technical Reference for SQL Server Views in System Center 2012 Configuration Manager
https://technet.microsoft.com/en-us/library/dn581974.aspx

SQL Server Views in System Center 2012 Configuration Manager
https://technet.microsoft.com/en-us/library/dn581978.aspx

Configuration Manager 2012 Hardware and Software Inventory Views
https://technet.microsoft.com/en-us/library/dd334670.aspx

Creating Custom Reports By Using Configuration Manager 2007 SQL Views
http://www.microsoft.com/en-us/download/details.aspx?id=22052

Note: The Configuration Manager 2007 SQL Views documentation is still relevant to much of what is contained within Configuration Manager 2012. This is a perfect example of views remaining usable with version updates. Within this documentation is a very useful *.chm help file, a Visio diagram of the view relationships, and Excel spreadsheet of available views with column names. Highly recommended!

Chapter 4

Report Authoring Tools

There are two report authoring tools that I discuss in this chapter. One is the Report Builder utility, and the second is SQL Server Data Tools, formerly known as Business Intelligence Development Studio. This chapter provides an overview of these utilities, including background on making the appropriate selection of whether to use Report Builder or SQL Server Data Tools.

Note: SSRS reports are stored with an *.RDL file type, which stands for report definition file. Further, all SSRS report definitions are stored as XML files.

SQL Server 2012 Report Builder

SQL Server 2012 Report Builder (same binaries as Report Builder 3.0) is a report development utility that is compatible and integrated with SQL Server 2008 R2 and SQL Server 2012 SSRS. It has a ribbon interface and a report builder wizard that assists in report creation. Further, it can be used to modify existing reports.

Here are the methods to run or install SQL Server 2012 Report Builder:

- From the SSRS Report Manager menu interface, the Report Builder utility can be started as a Click-to-Run application. Another technique is to select a report that you wish to modify, choose the report properties, and then click Modify. Report Builder will then start, allowing you to modify the report

- You can download and install the SQL Server 2012 Report Builder *.msi-based utility. The advantage of this approach is that you can edit report definition files that have been saved locally. This is useful for offline development.

An example of the SQL Server 2012 Report Builder Getting Started interface is shown next:

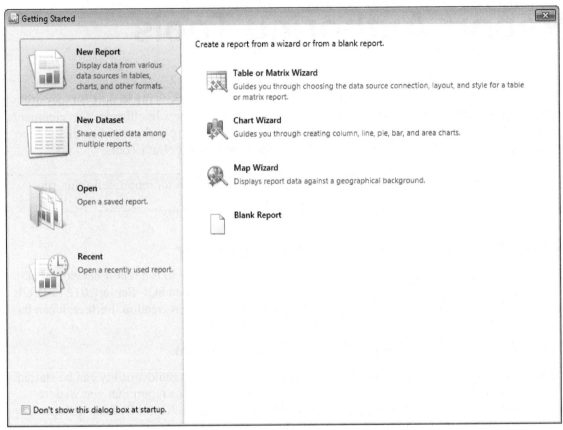

The SQL Server 2012 Report Builder Getting Started wizard-like interface.

The primary SQL Server 2012 Report Builder interface is shown next:

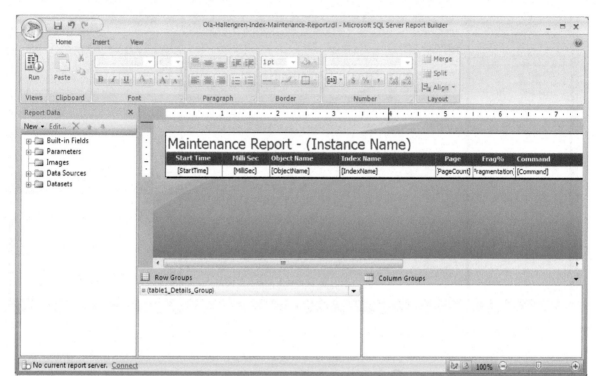

The SQL Server 2012 Report Builder interface.

SQL Server Data Tools

SQL Server Data Tools contains a rich collection of graphical query and designer interfaces that allow the development of a complete reporting solution. It a subset of the Visual Studio development environment.

SQL Server Data Tools is installed as an optional component of SQL Server and is displayed and enabled as SQL Server Data Tools. Additionally, this utility is available as a separate download from Microsoft (see the "Resources" section at the end of this chapter for more information).

A sample SQL Server Data Tools report project is shown next. Note the Solution Explorer and Properties windows on right, the menu bar and Report Data window items, shown on the left. Not shown is a rich toolbox for custom report development.

Note: The report development Toolbox can be accessed; from the menu by clicking View > Toolbox or from keyboard by using shortcut Ctrl-Alt-X.

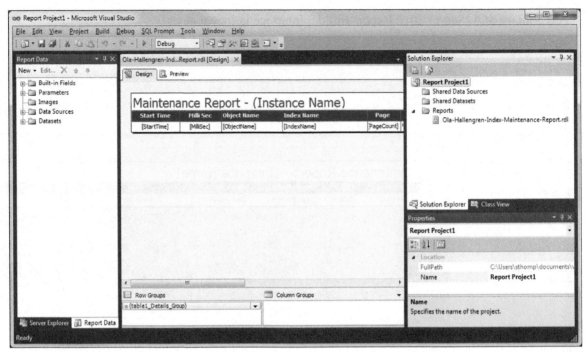

The SQL Server Data Tools interface.

Compare and Contrast

In order to make the determination of which development platform to use, let's consider the advantages of each report development utility by comparing and contrasting.

SQL Server 2012 Report Builder	SQL Server Data Tools
Primarily a client tool for end users	Primary target users are report developers
Edit a single report at a time	Edit multiple reports at a time
Difficult to work with linked reports	Easy to work with linked reports
Utility does not need to be installed	Utility does need to be installed
Not possible to deploy an entire reporting solution	Entire reporting solution can be deployed at one time
Not possible to work with Analysis Server Cubes or SSIS packages	Can be used to develop Analysis Server Cubes or SSIS packages
Shared datasets from report server	Shared datasets from project
Cannot use local shared datasets	Can use local shared datasets
N/A	Can import existing reports into the solution

SQL Server 2012 Report Builder	SQL Server Data Tools
N/A	Can copy/paste items between reports
Harder to access all report item properties	Report item properties fully exposed
XML view of RDL not possible	XML view of RDL readily available
N/A	Source control support available
N/A	Intellisense available for expressions

Recommendations

Either utility can be used to create and modify existing reports.

For some end users, SQL Server 2012 Report Builder may be the best choice for occasional report creation or report enhancement. It is built into the core SSRS Report Manager interface and is fairly intuitive.

SQL Server Data Tools is the ideal solution for serious report development. It has many strengths as outlined in the previous table. You can create a complete SQL Server Data Tools reporting solution that can deployed to a test environment for certification. Once certified in test, the *same solution* can be deployed to production. Another advantage, in addition to the reports deployed to SSRS, you automatically have a backup of your custom reports on your local file system.

Real World Note: There are times this author has used SQL Server 2012 Report Builder to quickly build a single report and then imported that report into SQL Server Data Tools. In that way, the custom reports can be managed within one, complete reporting solution.

Resources

The following resources are useful articles from Microsoft and other community sources as appropriate:

Comparing Report Authoring Environments
https://technet.microsoft.com/en-us/library/dd207010(v=sql.105).aspx

Microsoft SQL Server Data Tools - Business Intelligence for Visual Studio 2012
http://www.microsoft.com/en-us/download/details.aspx?id=36843

Microsoft® SQL Server® 2012 Report Builder
http://www.microsoft.com/en-us/download/details.aspx?id=29072

Chapter 5

Customizing and Modifying Existing Reports

In this chapter, you explore how to use SQL Server 2012 Report Builder. As a practical exercise, you use an existing report and add a company logo, add a new column, and explore the interactive features contained within SQL Server 2012 Report Builder.

Step-by-Step Guide Requirements

If you want to follow the step-by-step guides in this chapter, you need a lab environment configured as outlined in Chapter 1, have configured Reporting Services in Chapter 2, and have installed SQL Server Management Studio on PC0001 in Chapter 3. In this chapter, you use the following virtual machines:

DC01   CM01   PC0001

The VMs used in this chapter.

You also need to have downloaded the following software:

SQL Server 2012 Report Builder

Install SQL Server 2012 Report Builder

In these steps, I assume you have downloaded the following software to **PC0001**.

- **SQL Server 2012 Report Builder.** Copied to **C:\Setup\SQL2012RB**.

- **Book sample files.** Copied to **C:\Setup**.

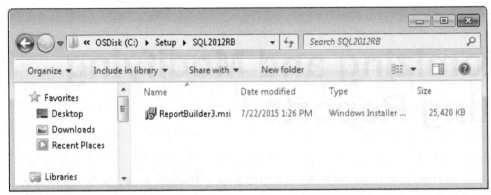

The SQL Server 2012 Report Builder *.msi file, downloaded from Microsoft and saved to the C:\Setup\SQL2012RB folder.

Complete the following steps to install SQL Server 2012 Report Builder:

1. On **PC0001**, log on as **VIAMONSTRA\Administrator**.

2. Open an elevated **PowerShell** prompt, and install **SQL Server2012 Report Builder** by running the following command:

    ```
    msiexec /i C:\Setup\SQL2012RB\ReportBuilder3.msi /qb
    ```

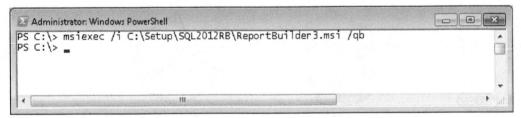

Installing SQL Server 2012 Report Builder.

3. When the **SQL Server 2012 Report Builder** setup is complete, click the start button in the lower left corner and confirm that the **Report Builder 3.0 icon** appears in the Start menu.

4. Exit the elevated **PowerShell** prompt.

Configure Internet Explorer for SSRS

For any client that needs to access and run SSRS, you need to configure Internet Explorer to properly access SSRS.

1. On **PC0001**, log on as **VIAMONSTRA\Administrator**.

2. Start **Internet Explorer** and enter **http://cm01.corp.viamonstra.com/reports**.

3. You are prompted for credentials because Internet Explorer believes this is an Internet connection. Cancel the prompt for credentials. Then to correct, from the **Internet Explorer** toolbar, click **Tools / Internet Options / Security**. In the **Select a zone** area, select **Local Internet**, and then click **Sites**.

Note: Alternatively, you could use the Server NETBIOS name CM01 as a workaround.

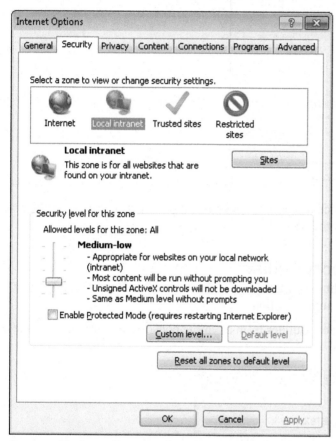

Internet Explorer Internet Options.

4. Click **Advanced**. Click **Add** to add the http://cm01.corp.viamonstra.com SSRS URL to the local intranet website.

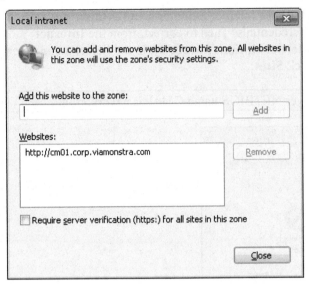

Internet Explorer—Local intranet zone.

5. Click **Close**, and click **OK** twice to return to **Internet Explorer**. If necessary, refresh the browser, and you should have the SSRS home directory displayed.

Import Certificate for Report Builder

As a one-time setup, if you wish to edit existing data sets (queries) within Report Builder, you need to import a certificate for secure authentication.

If you do not, and you need to run Report Builder from a remote console, you are likely to see the following error message:

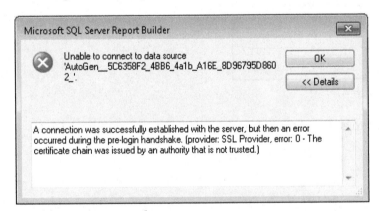

Unable to connect to data source error message.

To fix this issue you need to complete the following two procedures.

Export the Required Certificate

1. On **CM01**, log on as **VIAMONSTRA\Administrator**.

2. Click **Start / Run**, type in **certlm.msc**, and press **Enter**.

3. Expand **Personal / Certificates**, and select the certificate with the name of the server (Friendly Name: **ConfigMgr SQL Server Identification Certificate**).

4. Right-click the **certificate**, select **All Tasks**, and then select **Export**.

5. On the **Welcome to the Certificate Export Wizard** page, click **Next**.

6. On the **Export Private Key** page, select **No, do not export the private key** and click **Next**.

7. On the **Export File Format** page, select **DER encoded binary X.509 (.CER)** and click **Next**.

8. On the **File to Export** page, click **Browse**, and save the file to **C:\Setup**. Name the file **CM01-SSRS.cer**, click **Save**, and then click **Next**.

9. Click **Finish**, and then click **OK**.

Import the Certificate on the Remote Computer

1. On **PC0001**, log on as **VIAMONSTRA\Administrator**.

2. Start the **MMC console** with administrative rights.

Note: The certlm.msc MMC is not available for Windows 7.

3. From the menu bar, click **File / Add or Remove Snap-ins**. Select the **Certificates** snap-in, click **Add**, and then select the **Computer account** option. Click **Next**, choose the default **Local Computer**, click **Finish**, and then click **OK**.

4. Expand **Certificates / Trusted Root Certification Authorities / Certificates**.

5. Right-click **Certificates**, select **All Tasks**, and then select **Import.**

6. On the **Welcome to the Certificate Import Wizard** page, click **Next**.

7. On the **File to Import** page, click **Browse**, locate the certificate you exported in the preceding export procedure (**\\CM01\C$\Setup\CM01-SSRS.cer**), and click **Next**.

8. On the **Certificate Store** page, verify that **Trusted Root Certification Authorities** is selected and click **Next**.

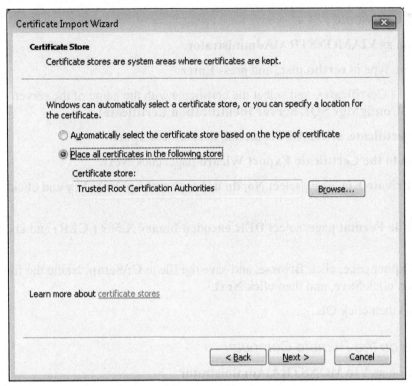

The Certificate Import Wizard.

9. On the **Completing the Certificate Import Wizard** page, click **Finish**.

10. You should receive the message "The import was successful." Click **OK**.

You should now be able to create your reports from **PC0001**. This process needs to be repeated from any other computer that will use Report Builder.

Note: Thanks to Ronni Pedersen (MVP) for documenting this process.

Edit a Report with Report Builder

In this section, you add a custom logo to your report.

For any client that needs to access and run SSRS, you need to configure Internet Explorer to properly access SSRS.

1. On **PC0001**, log on as **VIAMONSTRA\Administrator**.

2. Start **Internet Explorer**, enter **http://cm01.corp.viamonstra.com/reports**.

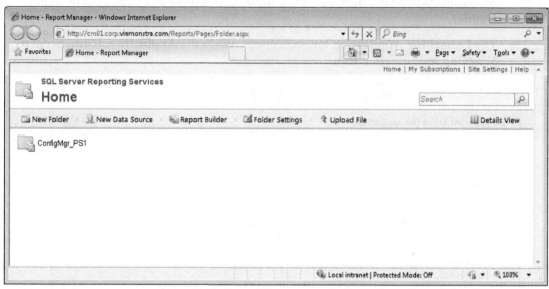

The SSRS Home page.

3. Click the home folder **ConfigMgr_PS1**. Note each of the folders contains reports of like categories. Select and click the folder **Hardware - General**.

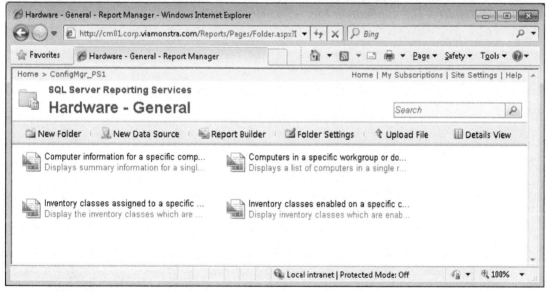

SSRS—Hardware – General folder.

4. Now, add a logo to the **Computers in a specific workgroup or domain** report. Click the report, and then on the right side, click the drop-down list and click **Edit in Report Builder**.

5. The **Launching Application** message opens. When the **Application Run - Security Warning** appears, click **Run**.

Report Builder—The Application Run – Security Warning.

After a few moments, the SQL Server 2012 Report Builder downloads and runs.

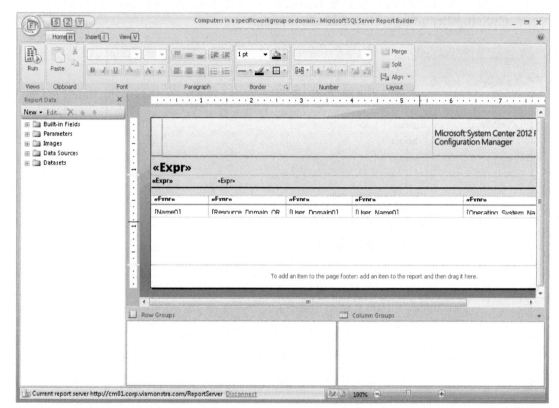

Report Builder—Report Builder.

6. On the Report Builder toolbar, click the **Insert** tab, and then click **Image**. Then, starting in the upper left corner of the report layout, click and hold the mouse button to expand the image to cover the title section to the left of the "Microsoft System Center 2012 R2 Configuration Manager" label. When you release the mouse button, the **Image Properties** dialog box appears.

7. For the **Use this image** option, click **Import**, select **PNG files** in the drop-down list, and select the ViaMonstra logo (**ViaMonstra_Report_Header.png**, available in **C:\Setup\Branding**). Click **OK** to use image.

Report Builder—The Image Properties dialog box.

8. Click **OK**, and you should see your selected image in the upper left corner of the report.

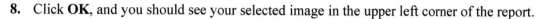

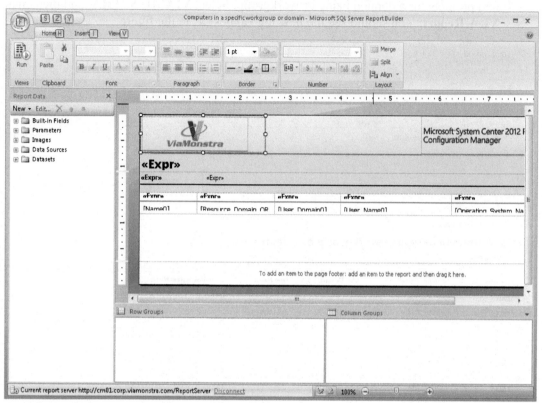

Report Builder after adding a custom image.

9. To test the revision, in the **Home** tab, click **Run**. Report Builder connects to SQL Server and prompts for a domain name or workgroup. Select **VIAMONSTRA**, and then click **View Report**. You should see the new logo appear as in the figure.

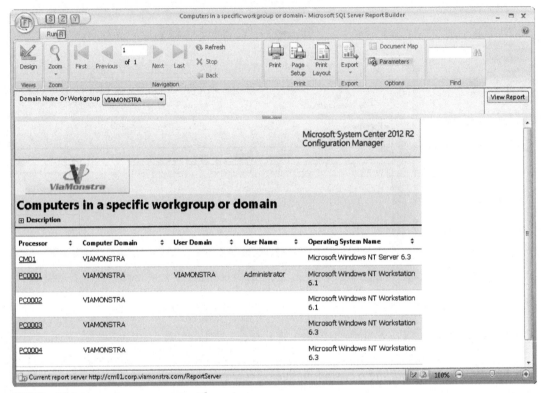

SSRS—Using a custom report with an image.

10. Click the **Design** button (in the upper left) to return to Report Builder Edit mode.

11. When you are satisfied with the changes, click the **Report Builder** button (upper left) and then click **Save**.

The Report Builder Save Option.

Alternatively, you could select the **Save As** option to save a local copy of the report definition.

Note: This type of interactive design and run to test changes is great way to immediately view the changes. At this point, none of the changes made, or yet stored on SSRS or saved. Using the Save As to store a report copy locally or on a server share is convenient way to maintain a backup of your custom reports.

Add a Column to a Report

In this section, you add a new column to an existing report. Further, you learn more about *datasets*. Datasets are used with Report Builder to retrieve data from SQL Server and populate the report. Behind the scenes, a dataset uses a properly formatted query (or stored procedure) and a *data source name* (DSN) to make this happen. A DSN is essentially a pointer to the SQL Server and database that will be accessed and the appropriate security credentials.

1. You need to add another field, **AD Site Name**, to the **Computers in a specific workgroup or domain** report. On the left side of the Report Builder editor, expand the **Datasets** node.

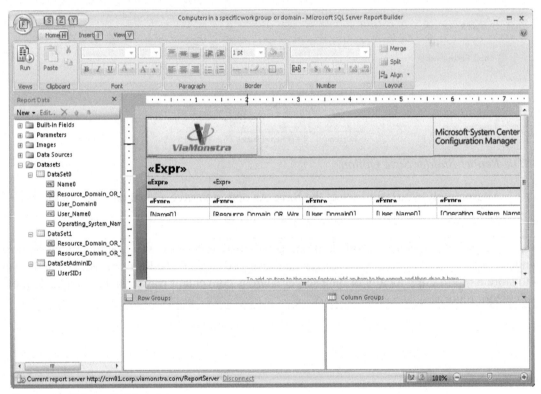

Report Builder—Editing datasets.

2. Right-click **Dataset0** and select **Dataset Properties.**

Report Builder—Dataset Properties.

3. Click **Query Designer**. When prompted for **Enter Data Source Credentials**, enter **P@ssw0rd** for **Password**, and then click **OK**.

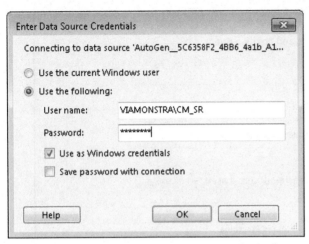

Report Builder—Enter Data Source Credentials.

4. Edit the query by adding the new field **SYS.AD_Site_Name0**, (also add a "," on the end of the "SYS.Operating_System_Name_and0" line) click **OK**, and then click **OK** again to close the **Dataset Properties** window. When complete, the SQL statement should appear as follows:

```
SELECT DISTINCT SYS.Name0,SYS.Resource_Domain_OR_Workgr0,
                SYS.User_Domain0,SYS.User_Name0,
                SYS.Operating_System_Name_and0,
                SYS.AD_Site_Name0
FROM fn_rbac_R_System(@UserSIDs)  SYS
WHERE SYS.Resource_Domain_OR_Workgr0 LIKE @variable
AND (Client_Type0 =1
OR (Client_Type0 IS NULL AND EAS_DeviceID IS NULL))
ORDER BY SYS.Resource_Domain_OR_Workgr0, SYS.Name0
```

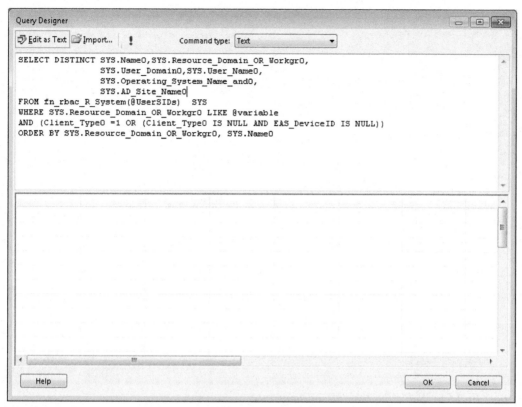

Report Builder—Query Designer with the modified SQL statement.

5. Select the column header for **Operating_System_Name_and0**, right-click, and select **Insert column to right**.

67

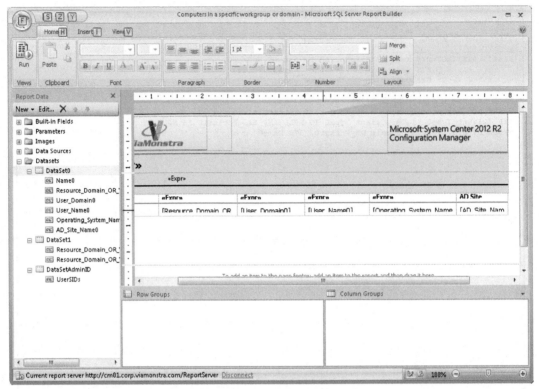

Report Builder—Selecting the data column.

6. Adjust the width for the columns so they all fit under the report header.

7. Select the new column on the right, select the column head and enter **AD Site** for the column header. In the data cell, below the header, click the small icon in the upper right of the cell, and then select **AD_Site_Name0**.

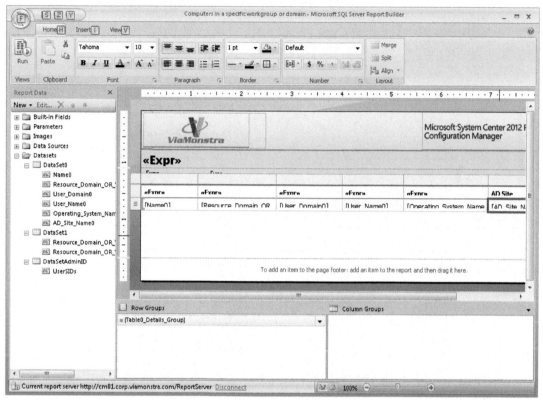

Report Builder—Adding a new data column.

8. Click **Run** to view the modified report.

9. When you are satisfied with the changes, click the **Report Builder** button, and then click
    Save.

Note: I recommend saving a copy of any modified report, as a subsequent Configuration Manager
Service Pack update may replace any custom report that has been created. The next chapter
discusses techniques for preventing custom reports from being replaced.

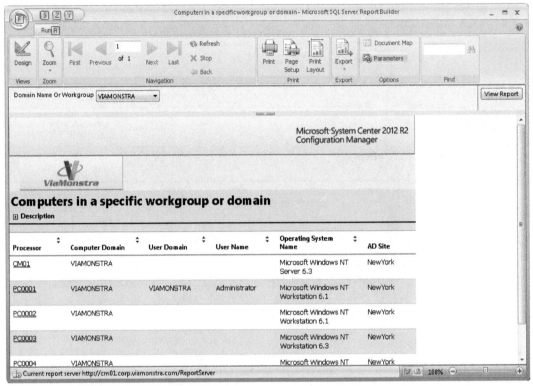

Report Builder—The report with a new column.

Summary

As demonstrated in this chapter, SQL Server 2012 Report Builder may be the best choice for occasional report creation or report enhancement. After you are familiar with the utility, you can use it to quickly modify an existing report, or create a new report using the Report Wizard.

Resources

The following resources are useful articles from Microsoft and other community sources as appropriate.

Comparing Report Authoring Environments
https://technet.microsoft.com/en-us/library/dd207010(v=sql.105).aspx

Editing a Report Dataset from a remote console
http://www.ronnipedersen.com/2014/12/sql-report-builder-unable-to-connect-to-data-source/

Chapter 6

Creating Reports

In this chapter, you create reports using SQL Server Data Tools. You learn how to navigate the SQL Server Data Tools environment. As a practical exercise, you create and deploy a new reporting solution with custom reports.

Step-by-Step Guide Requirements

If you want to follow the step-by-step guides in this chapter, you need a lab environment configured as outlined in Chapter 1, have configured Reporting Services in Chapter 2, and have installed SQL Server Management Studio on PC0001 in Chapter 3. In this chapter, you use the following virtual machines:

DC01   CM01   PC0001

The VMs used in this chapter.

You should have the following software installed on PC0001:

- SQL Server Management Studio
- SQL Server Data Tools

> **Note**: If you used the setup process for SQL Server Management Studio in Chapter 3, you are all set!

Configuring SQL Server Data Tools

After you have installed SQL Server Management Studio and the Data Tools option, you have everything you need to begin.

Upon first use, the SQL Server Data Tools environment needs to be configured for the reporting solution. The framework for the SQL Server Data Tools environment is based on the Visual Studio 2010 shell.

Create a Report with SQL Server Data Tools

In addition to configuring the SQL Server Data Tools, you explore the use of the Report Wizard to deploy your first report.

Complete the following steps to configure SQL Server Data Tools:

1. On **PC0001**, log on as **VIAMONSTRA\Administrator**.

2. Click **Start**, expand **Microsoft SQL Server 2012**, and click **SQL Server Data Tools.**

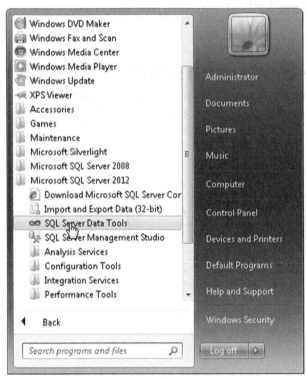

Starting SQL Server Data Tools.

3. Select **Business Intelligence Settings**, and click **Start Visual Studio**.

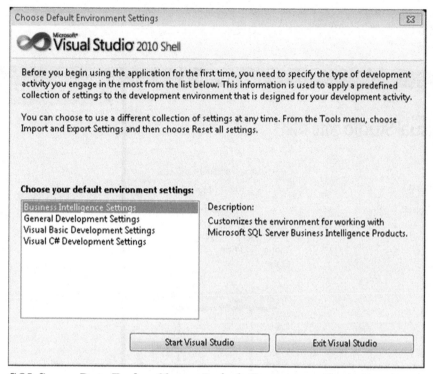

SQL Server Data Tools—Choose Default Environment Settings.

4. Click **New Project**.

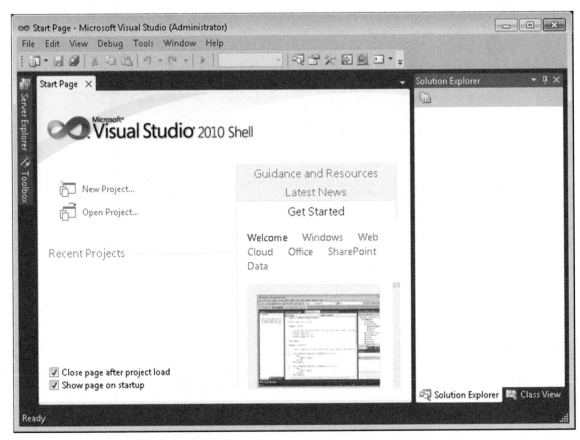

SQL Server Data Tools—Start Page.

5. Select **Report Server Project Wizard**: then after **Name**, type **PracticalReports**, and
click **OK.**

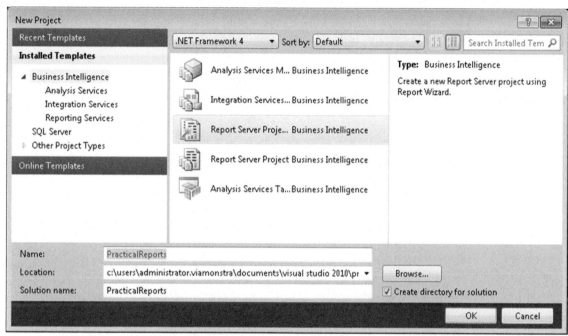

SQL Server Data Tools—Selecting a New Project template.

6. On the **Welcome to the Report Wizard** page, click **Next**.

7. On the **Select the Data Source** page, in the **Name** textbox, type in **CMPS1**, and then
click **Edit**.

8. In the **Connection Properties** window, after **Server name**, enter **CM01**; under **Log on to the server**, select **Use Windows Authentication**; under **Connect to a database**, select **CM_PS1** from the **Select or enter a database** drop-down list.

Connection Properties.

9. Click **Test Connection** to validate the data source credentials. You should be rewarded with success.

Connection test.

10. Click **OK** to save Connection Properties, select the **Make this a shared data source** check box, and then click **Next**.

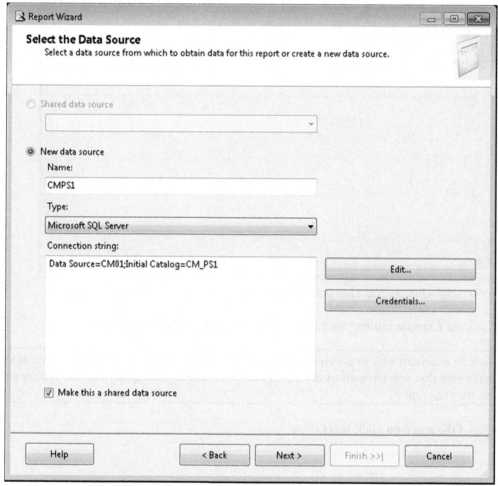

Report Wizard—Select or create a data source.

11. On the **Design the Query** page, click **Query Builder**, click **Edit as Text**, type the following query into the builder interface (you also can copy and paste from the Chapter/Ch6-1.sql file in the book sample files).

```
SELECT   sys.Netbios_Name0 AS ComputerName,
         sys.Resource_Domain_OR_Workgr0 AS Domain,
         sys.User_Name0 AS UserName,
         sys.Operating_system_Name_and0 AS OperatingSystem,
         sys.AD_Site_Name0 AS ADSiteName
FROM v_R_system_Valid  sys
ORDER BY sys.Netbios_Name0
```

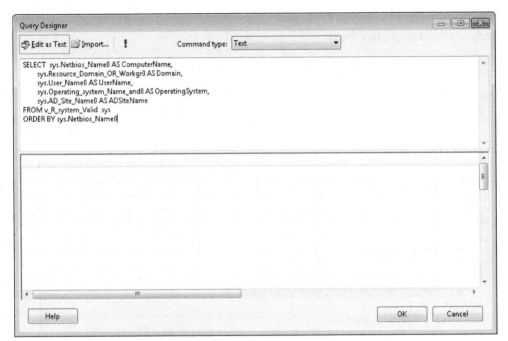

Report Wizard—Interactive Query Designer.

12. Click the **Execute** button (the red **!**) to execute query and view results.

Note: This is an excellent way to preview the results of a query. It is well worth your time at this point to make sure that you have all of the fields that you want in your query and the results are appropriate for your report.

---

13. Click **OK**, and then click **Next**.

Report Wizard—Design the Query.

14. On the **Select the Report Type** page, select **Tabular** and then click **Next**

Note: Matrix report layout option is available, as well.

15. On the **Design the Table** page, click the **Details** button to add all the available fields to the **Displayed fields** Details section, and then click **Next**.

> **Note**: This design interface allows you to display fields on a report in the following manner: Once per Page, Once per Group, or as a list (using Details). Often, the Group and Details are used in conjunction to list data within logical groupings. The order that the fields appear in these sections are the order in which they will appear on the report. Take the time now to get the order correct!

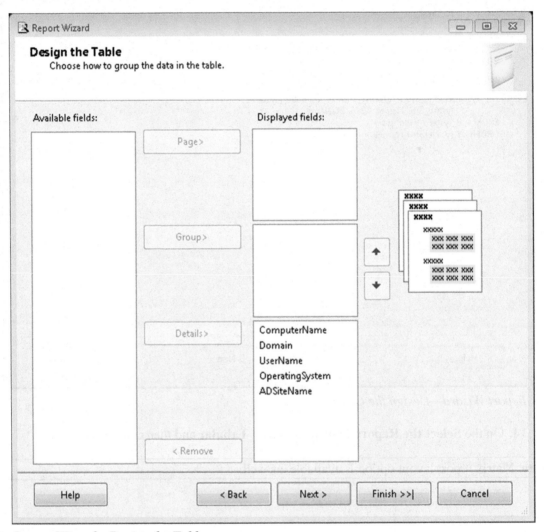

Report Wizard—Design the Table.

16. On the **Choose the Table Style** page, select **Corporate** and then click **Next**.

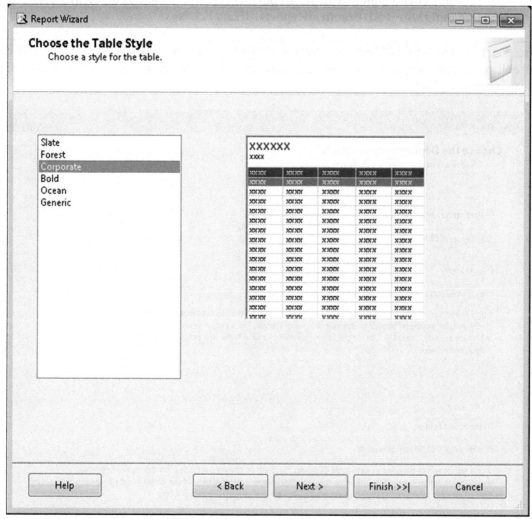

Report Wizard—Choose the Table Style.

17. On the **Choose the Deployment Location** page, in the **Report server** field, enter **http://cm01.corp.viamonstra.com/ReportServer**, and in the **Deployment folder** field, enter **/ConfigMgr_PS1/PracticalReports**. Then click **Next**.

Note: The report path for production instances of Configuration Manager depends on the site code in use. It is recommended to place your custom report folder beneath the default Configuration Manager reporting folder.

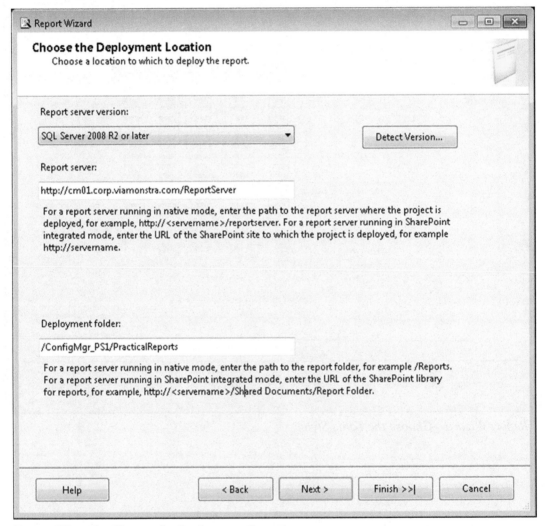

Report Wizard—Choose the Deployment Location.

18. On the **Completing the Wizard** page, for **Report name**, enter **Computer Operating System Information** and then click **Finish.**

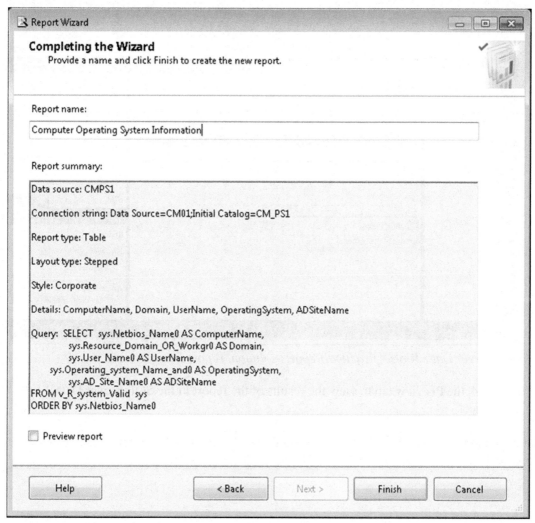

Report Wizard—Completing the Wizard.

The SQL Server Data Tools interface with the new report should display as follows:

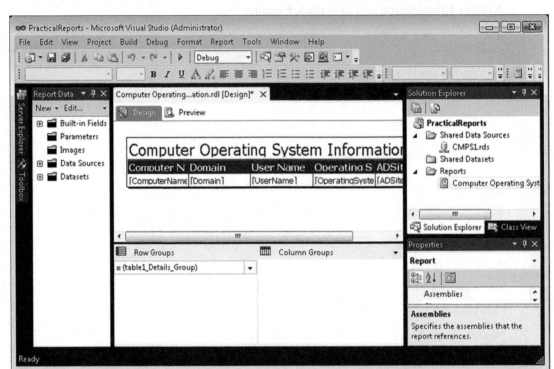

SQL Server Data Tools—PracticalReports solution, report Design view.

19. Click the **Preview** tab to view the results of the report in the SQL Server Data Tools project.

> **Note**: You may need to close the Solution and Properties views (on the left) to see the report. These features can be enabled or disabled by using the View menu.

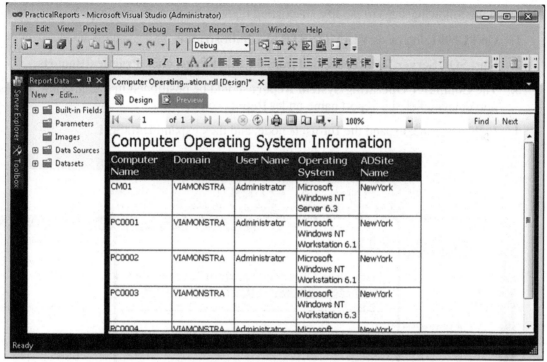

SQL Server Data Tools—PracticalReports solution, report Preview view.

20. Click **File / Save All** to save work in progress.

21. Close the **SQL Server Data Tools** solution, and if prompted, save any changes.

Note: At this point, you have successfully created your first SQL Server Data Tools solution, with a shared data set and one custom report. The report has not yet been deployed to the Reporting Server. This occurs in the "Deploy a Reporting Solution" section later in this chapter.

Modify a Report with SQL Server Data Tools

It is a fairly common practice to modify reports to add or remove data columns, or perhaps add report parameters (covered in the next chapter). In this section, you add a column to an existing report. This involves several steps, including adding the new field to the SQL query and then adding the field to the report.

In this practical example, you change the OperatingSystem data element to a more user-friendly name and add the ServicePack field to the existing report.

Note: This section is dependent on the previous sections being completed: Configuring SQL Server Data Tools and Creating a Report.

Complete the following steps to modify an existing report with SQL Server Data Tools:

1. On **PC0001**, log on as **VIAMONSTRA\Administrator**.

2. Start **SQL Server Data Tools**, and from the **Start Page**, click **PracticalReports**.

3. The **Computer Operating System Report** should be positioned in Design view. If it is not, double-click this report name under **Reports** on the right.

4. In the left pane, expand the **Datasets** node, and then expand **DataSet1**.

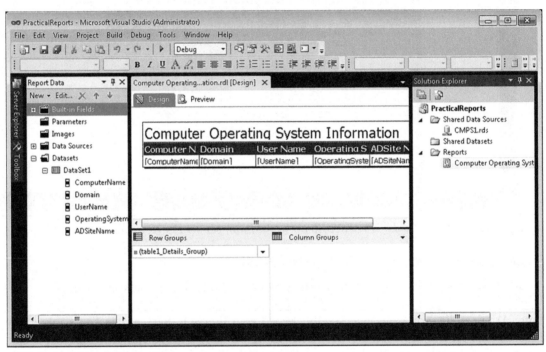

SQL Server Data Tools—Datasets.

5. Right-click **DataSet1**, click **Dataset Properties**, and the click **Query Designer**.

6. Type the following query into the **Query Designer Editor** (you also can copy and paste from the Chapter6/Ch6-2.sql file in the book sample files):

```
SELECT  sys.Netbios_Name0 AS ComputerName,
        sys.Resource_Domain_OR_Workgr0 AS Domain,
        sys.User_Name0 AS UserName,
        os.Caption0 AS OperatingSystem,
        os.CSDVersion0 AS ServicePack,
        sys.AD_Site_Name0 AS ADSiteName
FROM v_R_system_Valid  sys
INNER JOIN v_GS_OPERATING_SYSTEM os
        ON os.ResourceID = sys.ResourceID
ORDER BY sys.Netbios_Name0
```

> **Note**: You are joining the v_R_System_Valid view to the v_GS_OPERATING_SYSTEM view to retrieve the user-friendly name for operating system and to add the new Service Pack field. Additionally, because you have kept the same view alias name for the OperatingSystem, the report column will not have to be modified for this change to be reflected!

7. On the **Query Designer** tool bar, click the **Execute** button (!) to execute and test the query revision.

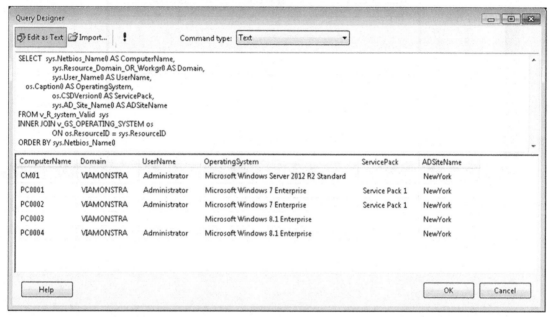

Query Designer.

8. Click **OK** twice to update the **Dataset Properties** window.

9. To insert a new column for the Service Pack column, on the **Computer Operating System Report**, select the **Operating System** column header. **Right-click** the column header, select **Insert Column >**, and then click **Right**.

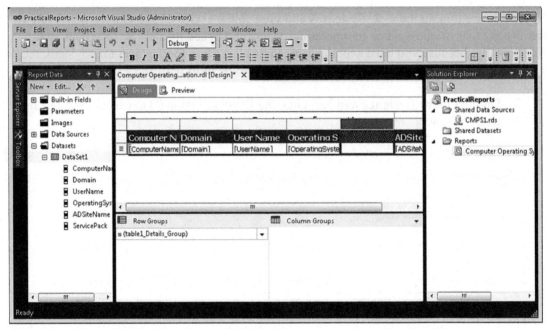

SQL Server Data Tools—Inserting a new column.

10. On the left side, click **ServicePack** and drag it to the empty cell to the right of Operating System.

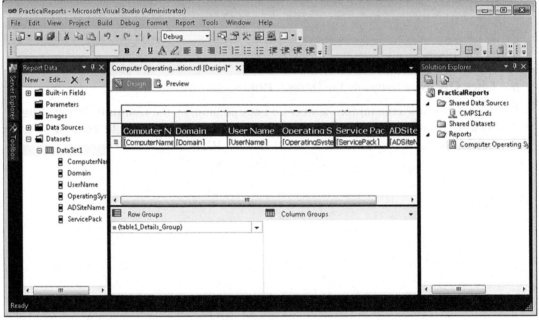

SQL Server Data Tools—Inserting the Service Pack column.

Note: The SQL Server Data Tools interface automatically adds the data portion and the column header.

11. From the SQL Server Data Tools menu bar, click **File / Save Computer Operating System Information.rdl As**.

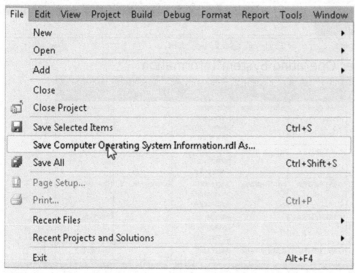

SQL Server Data Tools—Save As.

12. Change the file name (keep the remainder of the file path the same) to **Computer Operating System Detail.rdl**. Then, click **Save**.

13. Click the **Preview** tab to review the results of the report modification.

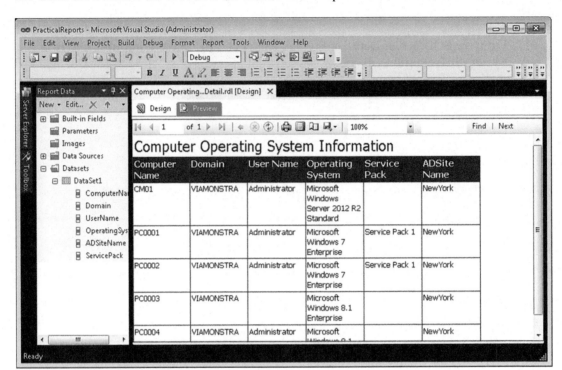

SQL Server Data Tools—The completed report.

Deploy a Reporting Solution

Up to this point, you have created a new report and made revisions to an existing report. By using the Save As feature, you created a second, more detailed report. In this section, you add a second report to the solution and then deploy the solution to SSRS.

Complete the following steps to add an existing report to SQL Server Data Tools and deploy a reporting solution:

1. On **PC0001**, log on as **VIAMONSTRA\Administrator**.

2. If it is not open from the last section, start **SQL Server Data Tools**, and from the **Start Page**, click **PracticalReports**.

3. On the right, in the **Solution Explorer**, right-click **Reports**, and select **Add / Existing Item**. Then select **Computer Operating System Information.rdl** and click **Add**.

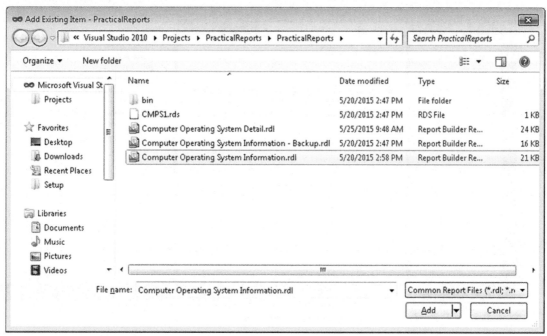

SQL Server Data Tools—Add Existing Item.

4. Verify that you now have two reports listed in the **Solution Explorer** under **Reports**.

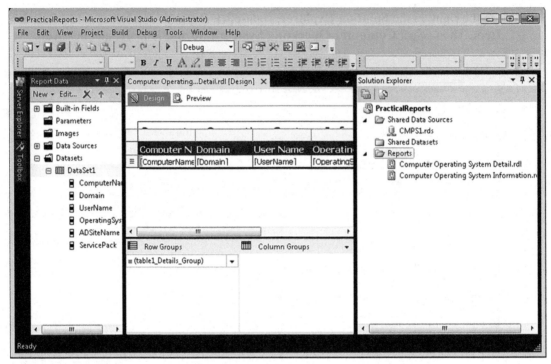

SQL Server Data Tools—with second added Report.

Real World Note: Adding an existing report item is an excellent way to import, manage, and integrate custom reports into a single reporting solution. These existing reports can be built using other tools, such as the SQL Server Report Builder. Typically, the only change required after import is to update the dataset to use the SQL Server Data Tools Shared Data Sources.

5. From the menu bar, click **Build / Build Practical Reports**. Verify that the build succeeded, with "Build succeeded" displayed in lower left of interface.

Note: The Build step verifies that the project is complete and no serious issues were found that could prevent a deployment.

6. From the menu bar, click **Build / Deploy Practical Reports**. You see the Deploy started... message and then Ready. Expanding the **Output** window, you can review the results of the Deploy task.

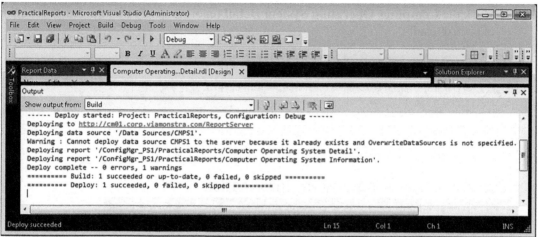

SQL Server Data Tools—Output task.

Note: Review the deployment output. The key line is the last line: Deploy: 1 succeeded, 0 failed, 0 skipped.

7. To verify the correct reporting solution deployment, start **Internet Explorer** and navigate to **http://cm01.corp.viamonstra.com/Reports**.

8. Click the **ConfigMgr_PS1** folder, and then browse to and click the **PracticalReports** folder, which is shown here in **Tile View**:

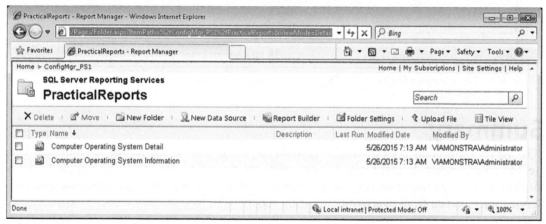

SSRS—The PracticalReports folder.

9. Click the **Computer Operating System Detail** report to verify that the report returns the expected results.

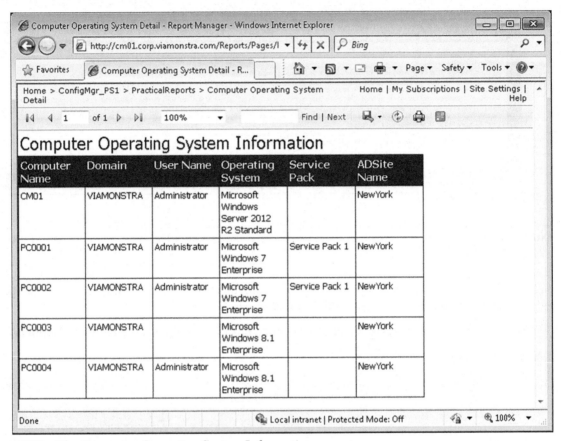

SSRS—The Computer Operating System Information report.

Summary

SQL Server Data Tools is a powerful way to create, build, and deploy reporting solutions. There are integrated wizards to assist with solution and report creation. By creating a unique folder name for the custom reporting solution, you potentially prevent a future Configuration Manager 2012 Service Pack update from overwriting existing reports.

Chapter 7

Advanced Reporting

In this chapter, you explore more practical examples of advanced reporting. You learn how to extend hardware inventory and then create a custom report for reporting on this information. Report parameters are implemented, as parameters provide the ability to filter and reduce the amount of information returned. Linked reports are created to illustrate another technique for reporting summary level data that enables drilling down to more detailed report information.

Step-by-Step Guide Requirements

If you want to follow the step-by-step guides in this chapter, you need a lab environment configured as outlined in Chapter 1, have configured Reporting Services in Chapter 2, and have installed SQL Server Management Studio on PC0001 in Chapter 3. In this chapter, you use the following virtual machines:

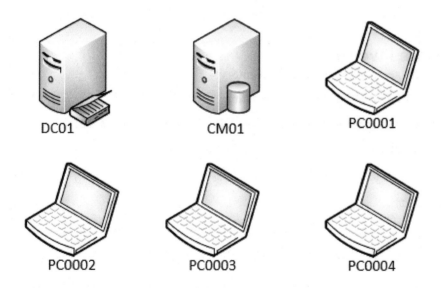

The VMs used in this chapter.

You should have the following software installed on PC0001:

- Configuration Manager 2012 Console
- Configuration Manager 2012 Console Cumulative Update Hotfix

- SQL Server Management Studio

- SQL Server Data Tools

Note: If you have not installed SQL Server Management Studio on PC0001, please review the setup process in Chapter 3. Additionally, you need to set up SQL Server Data Tools for first use, as described in the beginning of Chapter 6.

Extending Hardware Inventory

In this practical example; you have been asked to provide a report that includes basic information about each computer. There is an existing report that captures most of what you need; however, this report is missing the free disk space information.

Upon investigation, you learn that Configuration Manager does not capture free disk space by default. You need to extend the Configuration Manager hardware inventory to capture the Free Space attribute.

This task is handled in two steps:

1. Extending the hardware inventory

2. Creating the Custom Hardware Inventory report

Extend the Hardware Inventory

Complete the following steps to extend the hardware inventory:

1. On **CM01**, log on as **VIAMONSTRA\Administrator**.

2. Using the **Configuration Manager console**, in the **Administration** workspace, select **Client Settings**.

3. On the ribbon, select **Create Custom Client Device Settings**. Assign a name of **CM-Workstations**, and in the settings list, select the **Hardware Inventory** check box.

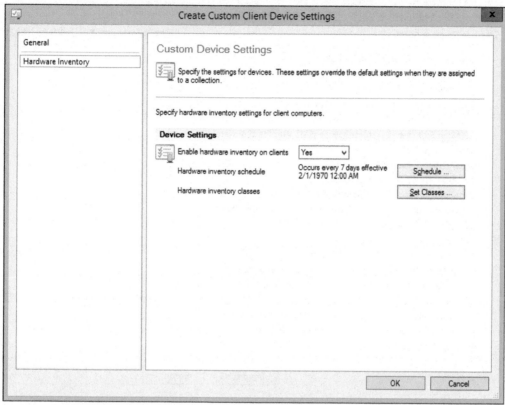

Hardware Inventory Custom Device Settings.

4. On left, click **Hardware Inventory**, and then click **Set Classes**.

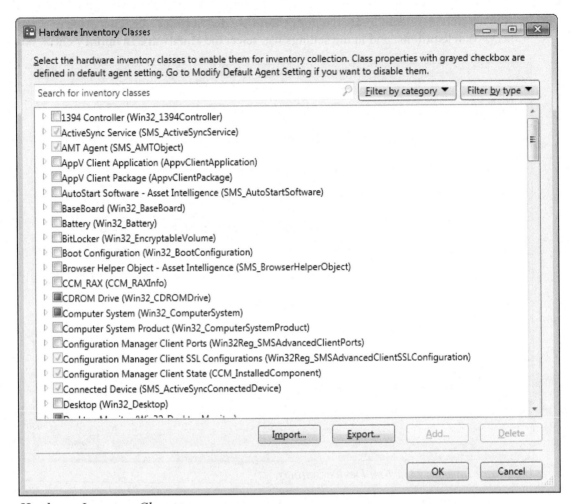

Hardware Inventory Classes.

Note: These hardware inventory classes correlate to the WMI classes available for the Configuration Manager Hardware Inventory process.

5. Browse to **Logical Disk (SMS_LogicalDisk)** class, enable **Free Space (MB)**, and then click **OK**. Click **OK** to close and save the changes for Custom Device Settings.

Note: Using the Hardware Inventory Class Filter can streamline the class location process. Entering "Disk" in the filter returns three classes. Additionally, you have the ability to filter by category or filter by type.

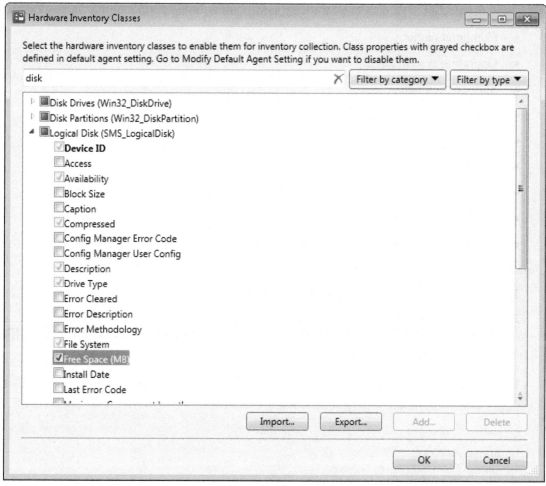

Hardware Inventory Classes—Logical Disk / Free Space (MB).

Real World Note: Be cautious in selecting only the inventory classes that you need to collect data and subsequently report. Better yet, enable only the attributes within the inventory class that you need more information. The reason for this recommendation is to prevent the database from bloating by collecting too much additional data. It is recommended to document custom inventory classes added and monitor database growth after making revisions.

6. Deploy the **CM-Workstations** custom client device settings to the **All Desktop and Server Clients** collection. On the next workstation hardware inventory cycle, data for the new **Free Space** attribute will be collected. Until then, the query results for Free Disk Space will appear as **NULL**.

Create the Custom Hardware Inventory Report

For this custom hardware inventory report, you have previously extended the hardware inventory to obtain information not collected by default.

You have been asked to provide the following information in this custom report for workstations:

- Computer name
- Operating system name
- Service pack name
- Processor type speed
- Total memory (MB)
- IP addresses
- Drive letter
- Total drive size (MB)
- Free space available (MB)

Follow these steps to create this report:

1. On **PC0001**, log on as **VIAMONSTRA\Administrator**.

2. Start **SQL Server Data Tools**, and from the **Start Page**, click **Open Project**. Then double-click the **PracticalReports** folder, select the **PracticalReports.sln** solution file, and click **Open**.

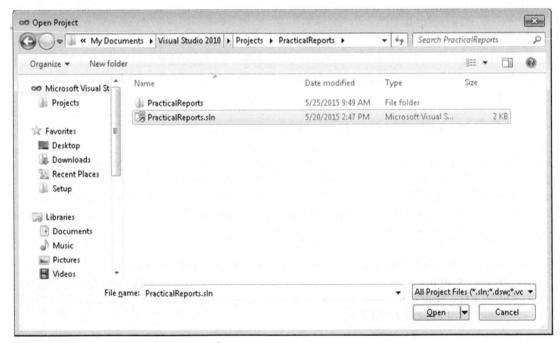

Open Project—PracticalReports solution.

3.   In the **Solution Explorer**, right-click **Reports** and then click **Add New Report.**

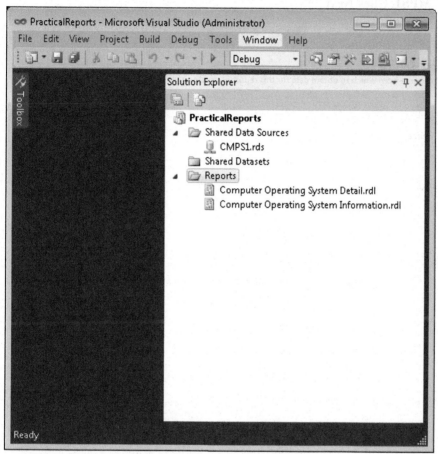

Solution Explorer—Add New Report.

4. On the **Welcome to the Report Wizard** page, click **Next**. Allow **Shared data source** to default to **CMPS1**. Click **Next**.

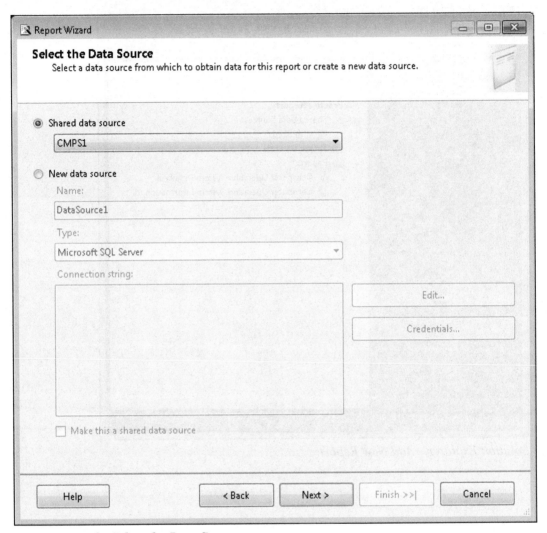

Report Wizard—Select the Data Source.

5. On the **Design the Query** page, type the following query into the **Query string** window (you also can copy and paste from the Chapter7/Ch7-1.sql file in the book sample files). Then click **Next**.

```sql
SELECT DISTINCT s.ResourceID,
     s.Netbios_Name0 AS ComputerName,
     os.Caption0 AS OperatingSystemName,
     os.CSDVersion0 AS ServicePack,
     pr.Name0 AS ProcessorTypeSpeed,
     m.TotalPhysicalMemory0 AS TotalMemoryMB,
     ip.IPAddress0 AS IPAddesses,
     ld.deviceid0 AS DriveLetter,
     ld.Size0 AS TotalDriveSizeMB,
     ld.freespace0 AS FreeSpaceAvaiableMB
FROM v_R_System_Valid s
INNER JOIN v_GS_OPERATING_SYSTEM os
     ON s.ResourceID = os.ResourceID
INNER JOIN v_GS_PROCESSOR pr ON s.ResourceID = pr.ResourceID
INNER JOIN v_GS_COMPUTER_SYSTEM gs
     ON s.ResourceID = gs.ResourceID
INNER JOIN v_GS_NETWORK_ADAPTER
     ON s.ResourceID = v_GS_NETWORK_ADAPTER.ResourceID
INNER JOIN v_GS_X86_PC_MEMORY m
     ON s.ResourceID = m.ResourceID
INNER JOIN v_GS_NETWORK_ADAPTER_CONFIGURATION ip
     ON s.ResourceID = ip.ResourceID
INNER JOIN v_GS_LOGICAL_DISK AS ld
     ON s.ResourceID = ld.ResourceID
WHERE  ip.IPAddress0 IS NOT NULL
     AND ip.DefaultIPGateway0 IS NOT NULL
     AND ld.DriveType0=3
     AND ld.deviceid0='C:'
AND s.Operating_System_Name_and0 LIKE '%Workstation%'
```

Note: Observe several things about this query: The DISTINCT keyword eliminates duplicate rows being returned and, in certain circumstances, is easier to use than the corresponding GROUP BY keyword. Each column alias uses Mixed Case capitalization, where the first letter of each word is capitalized, and there are no spaces in the column names. This naming convention assists in ensuring clear meaning of column names. And, the Report Wizard automatically creates spaces in the column name as part of the report creation process. There are a number of joins required in this query to combine all of the requested information in one result set. Each of the views is aliased as a best practice. Finally, the query criteria limits, or pre-qualifies, the information being returned to only workstation operating system, the logical C drive, and IP addresses that are valid. There is no ORDER BY in this query, as this can be managed in the report, as is shown later in this chapter.

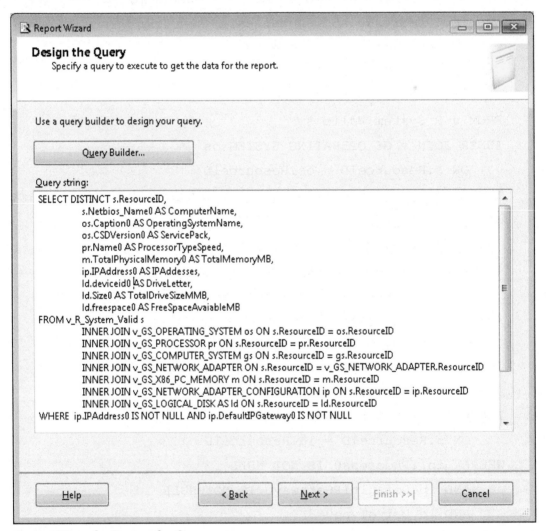

Report Wizard—Design the Query.

6. On the **Select the Report Type** page, set the report type to **Tabular** and click **Next**.

7. On the **Design the Table** page, add the available fields in order to **Details**, starting with the **ComputerName** and ending with **FreeSpaceAvailableMB** field. Click **Next**.

Note: Do not add the ResourceID field to the report. This field will be a hidden field within the dataset for the report. As such, it can be referenced within the report. For example, this field could be used to pass as a variable to a linked report. When possible, I recommend adding the ResourceID or MachineID to the core query.

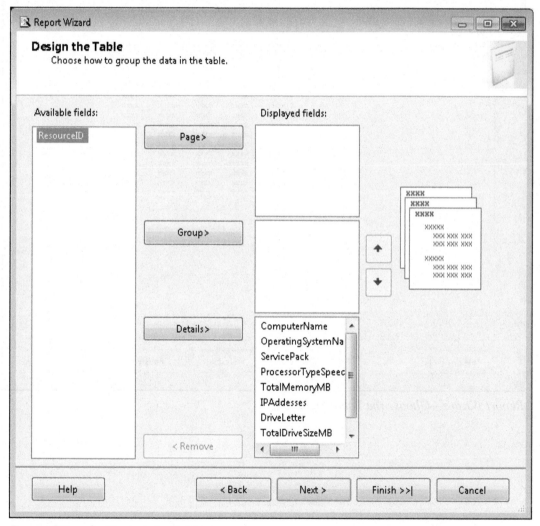

Report Wizard—Design the Table.

8. On the **Choose the Table Style** page, accept the default settings and click **Next**.

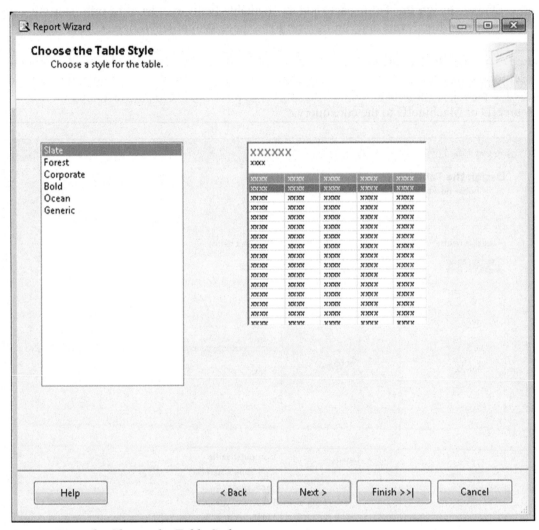

Report Wizard—Choose the Table Style.

9. On the **Completing the Wizard** page, name the report **Custom Hardware Inventory** and then click **Finish**.

Report Wizard—Naming the report.

10. In the **SQL Server Data Tools** interface, click **Preview** to view the results.

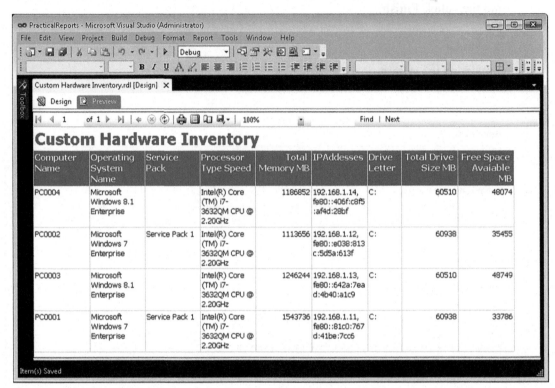

SQL Server Data Tools—Custom Hardware Inventory Preview.

Note: Often the report created by the Report Wizard is a good starting point. However, it needs additional work before it is ready to be published. This topic is discussed next.

Finalizing the Custom Hardware Inventory Report

In the preceding sections, you extended the hardware inventory to obtain information not collected by default. You also created a custom hardware inventory report to reflect this information.

The next steps involve enhancing the custom hardware inventory with the following:

- Adding default order
- Changing the font size for the report body
- Expanding and sizing columns appropriately
- Total memory column—changing the calculated size from KB to MB
- Adding interactive column sort

108

- Adding page numbers to the report

- Adding the date to the report

To complete these tasks, follow these steps:

1. On **PC0001**, log on as **VIAMONSTRA\Administrator**.

2. Start **SQL Server Data Tools**, and from the **Start Page**, click **Open Project**. Then double-click the **PracticalReports** folder, select the **PracticalReports.sln** solution file, and click **Open**.

Add Default Report Sort By

1. In the **Solution Explorer**, in the **Reports** section, select **Custom Hardware Information**, right-click it, and select **Open**.

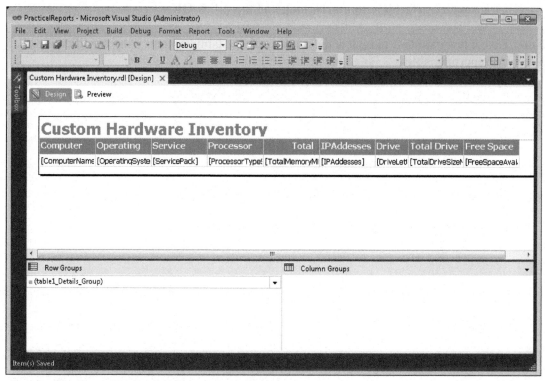

Custom Hardware Inventory Report—Design view.

Note: The Solution Explorer is hidden to show the full report. This report is used for the remainder of the "Finalizing the Custom Hardware Inventory Report" section.

2.   Select the **ComputerName** field, and then, to the left of the **ComputerName** field, right-click and select **Tablix Properties**.

Report Design View—Tablix Properties.

3.   In the left pane of the **Tablix Properties** dialog box, click **Sorting**; click the **Add** button; for **Sort by**, select **[ComputerName]**; and then click **OK**.

Note: Take a few moments to review the other available tablix options. Any modifications here affect the reporting tablix.

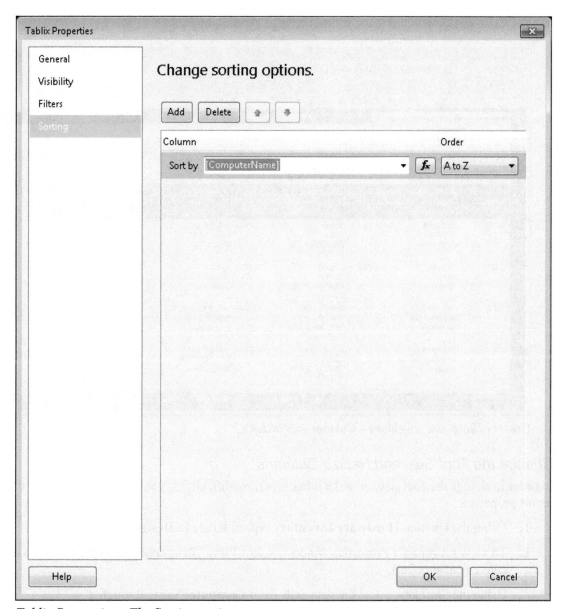

Tablix Properties—The Sorting option.

Real World Note: Adding a sort option to the tablix is a better approach, and more reliable than attempting to sort in a query. Do not use query sorts, as this imposes unnecessary resource overhead in retrieving data for the report!

4. Click **Preview** to test the sort order change by computer name.

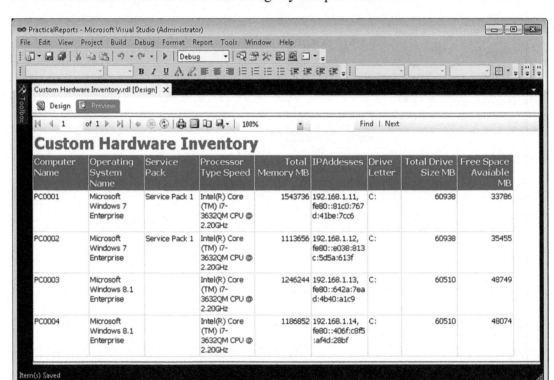

Custom Hardware Inventory—Custom sort order.

Change the Font Size and Resize Columns

In order to change the font size, or make other report modifications, you learn how to access the report properties.

1. Using the **Custom Hardware Inventory** report, toggle to **Design** view.

2. To view the report's Properties window, select **View / Properties Window** (hint: F4 is a convenient shortcut).

3. Using the Shift key, select the data cells from **ComputerName** through **FreeSpaceAvailableMB**.

4. In the **Properties** window, scroll down to locate and expand **Font,** and select **FontSize.**
Change **FontSize** to **8pt,** and **FontWeight** to **Bold.**

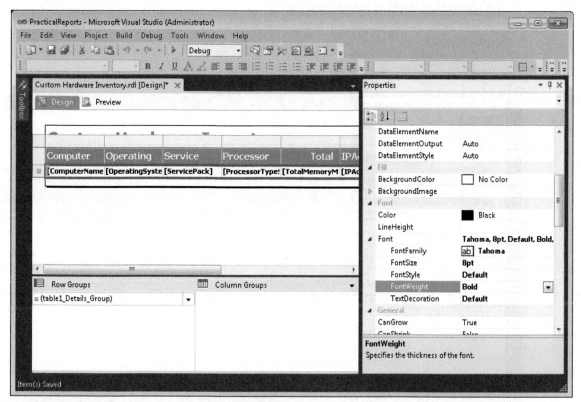

Custom Hardware Inventory—Properties Window.

5. Click **Preview** to view the results.

6.   Toggle the report to **Design** view. Select the Report Tablix. Similar to sizing an Excel spreadsheet, expand the height of the column header row, and then expand the width of the **Operating System Name** column.

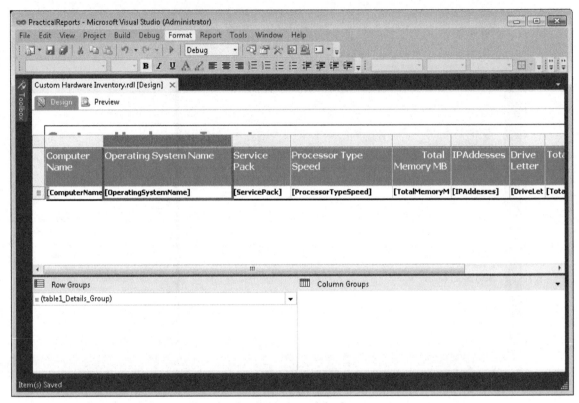

Custom Hardware Inventory—Font and columns modified.

7.   Custom Hardware Inventory—Resizing a column.

8.   Click **Preview** to view the results.

Note: Click Preview to check that the Operating System Name properly fits in the window. It may take several attempts to get the correct sizing. As you toggle from Design to Preview view, the report is saved automatically.

114

Use Expressions—Modify the Total Memory Column

Upon reviewing the Custom Hardware Inventory report, you notice that the Total Memory (MB) column is incorrectly showing the value as KB and needs to be modified. Now, you could change the derived field in the SQL query; however, it is useful to know how to manipulate data within the report.

1. Using the **Custom Hardware Inventory** report, toggle to **Design** view.

2. Select the data element **[TotalMemoryMB]**, right-click, and select **Expression**.

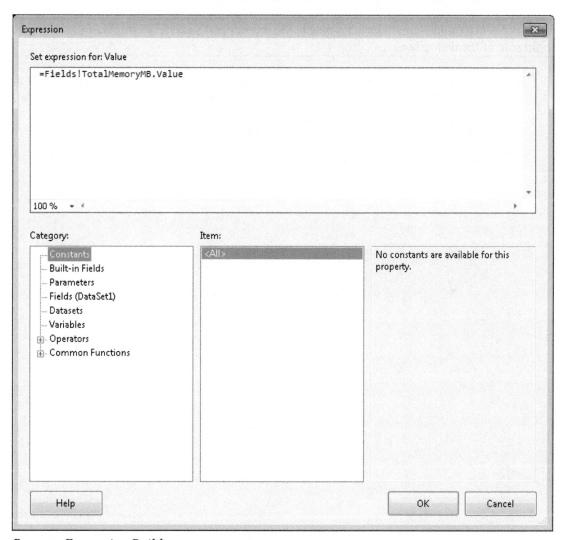

Report—Expression Builder.

3. Modify the expression as follows: **=Fields!TotalMemoryMB.Value / 1024**

4. Click **OK** to save changes.

Note: If you toggle to Preview view at this point, you'll notice that the resultant calculation has a number of values to the right of the decimal point. This requires formatting the numeric display.

---

5. Select the data element **[TotalMemoryMB]**, right-click, and select **Expression.**

6. In the **Category** list, expand **Common Functions** and select **Text**. In the **Item** list, select **FormatNumber**.

Note: For each of the items selected, you can see a description and an example of the item on the right side of the dialog box.

---

7. In **Set expression for: Value**, place the cursor to the right of the equal = symbol. In the **Item** list, double-click the **FormatNumber** item. To the right of the expression, type **, 0)**. The final expression for value should display **=FormatNumber (Fields!TotalMemoryMB.Value / 1024 , 0)**. Click **OK**.

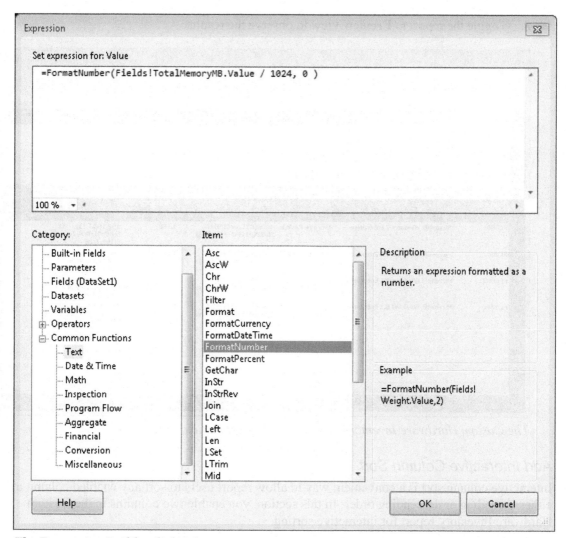

The Expression Builder dialog box.

Note: Using the Expression Builder dialog box is an excellent way to assist in creating expressions within your report. In the example you just completed, you created a calculated value that used one of the Format functions to properly display the number with 0 decimal places. With the included intellisense, it helps reduce mistakes creating custom expressions. You are not limited to using the builder interface. SQL Server Data Tools supports multiple expressions based on Visual Studio/VBScript-type functions. See the "Resources" section at the end of the chapter for more information on this topic.

8.   Toggle the report to **Preview** view to observe the results.

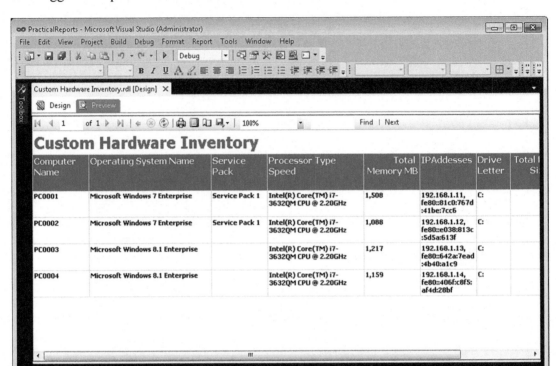

The Custom Hardware Inventory report with the custom field expression.

Add Interactive Column Sort

Interactive column sort is a convenient way to allow report users to sort any enabled column in either ascending or descending order. In this section, you enable two columns in the Custom Hardware Inventory report for interactive sorting.

1.   Using the **Custom Hardware Inventory** report, toggle to **Design** view.

2. Select the column header (blue background) for **Computer Name**. Right-click and select **Text Box Properties**.

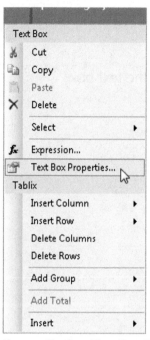

Report Tools—Text Box Properties.

3. In the **Text Box Properties** dialogs' left pane, click **Interactive Sorting**. Select the **Enable interactive sorting on this text box** check box. From the **Sort by** drop-down list, select **[ComputerName]**, and then click **OK**.

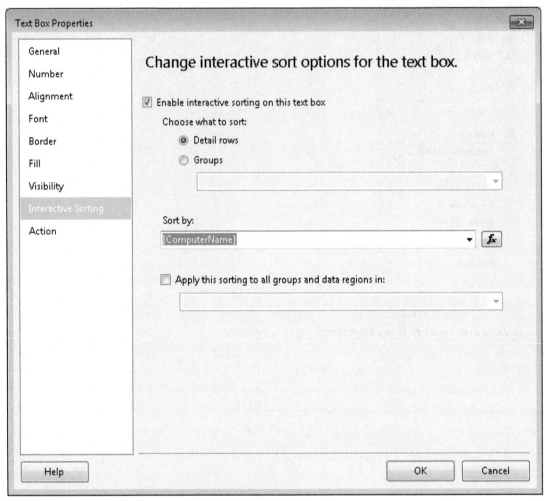

Text Box Properties—Enabling interactive sorting.

Note: Take the time to review the other exposed Text Box Properties. The Action element is demonstrated later in this chapter.

4. Select the column header for **Operating System Name** and repeat step 3, selecting **[OperatingSystemName]** from the **Sort by** drop-down list. Click **OK**.

5. Click **Preview** to view the results. In the upper right corner of the column headers for **Computer Name** and **Operating System Name**, click the **arrow symbol**.

Note: Clicking the column header arrow a second time changes the sort sequence from Ascending to Descending.

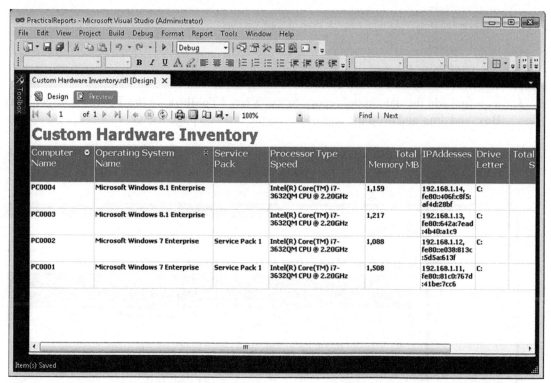

Custom Hardware Inventory report—Interactive sorting (Computer Name Descending).

Add Report Variables to Report

There are a number of built-in report variables available to assist in enhancing your reports. Two commonly used variables added to most reports are the date that the report was run and a page count.

You now add the date and page count to the Custom Hardware Inventory report.

1. Using the **Custom Hardware Inventory** report, toggle to **Design** view.

2. In the **Design** window, in the white space below the tablix, right-click and click **Add Page Footer**.

Note: Optionally, Add Page Footer is available from the menu bar: click Report and then select Add Page Footer.

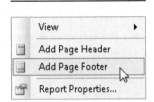

Report—Add Page Footer

3. You first add the date to the report. Select **View / Toolbox**. In the **Toolbox**, select **Text Box**, and drag and drop the text box onto the report's page footer.

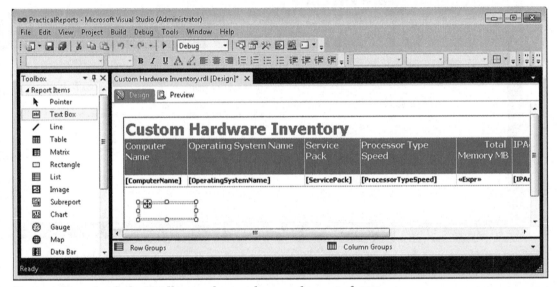

Report shown with the Toolbox and a text box on the page footer.

4. Right-click the new **text box** and select **Text Box Properties**. Perform the following steps:

    a. For **Name**, type **txtReportDate**.

    b. For **Value**, click the **Fx** symbol to the right of the drop-down list box to invoke the **Expression Builder**.

    c. In the **Expression** window, type = **"Execution Date: "** + **Globals!ExecutionTime**.

> **Note**: The execution time and many more variables can be found within the Expression Builder in Category: Built-in fields. Optionally, you can expand the width of the txtReportDate field.

    d. Click **OK** to close the **Expression Builder**, and then click **OK** to close the **Text Box Properties**.

Real World Note: It is always a best practice to name your custom text fields. It can make subsequent debugging easier, as attempting to find a text box named Textbox32 might be more challenging than a text box that has an appropriate name.

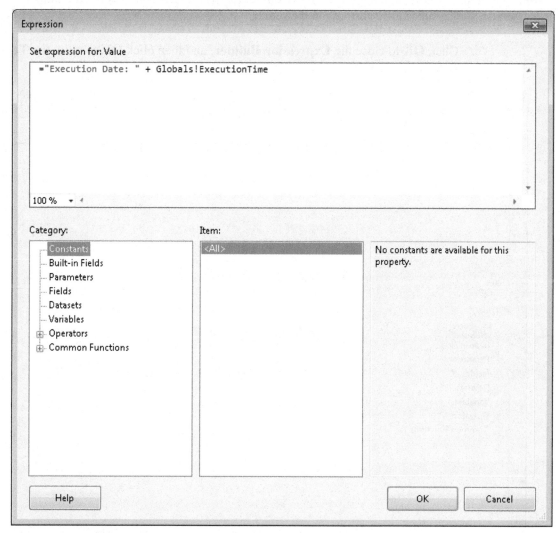

Expression Builder—Adding the execution time.

5. To add the page number to the report, from the **Toolbox**, select the **Text Box** control and drag and drop it on the report's page footer to the right of the report date text box.

6. Right-click the new **page number text box**, and then select **Text Box Properties**. Perform the following steps:

    a. For **Name**, type **txtPageNumber**.

    b. For **Value**, click the **Fx** symbol to the right of the drop-down list box to invoke the **Expression Builder**.

e.   In the **Expression** window, type **="Page " + CSTR(Globals!PageNumber) + "
of " + CSTR(Globals!TotalPages)**.

Note: This is an example of using the CSTR (Convert to String) function to convert a numeric
value to a string for subsequent display on the report.

c.   Click **OK** to close the **Expression Builder**, and then click **OK** to close the **Text
Box Properties**.

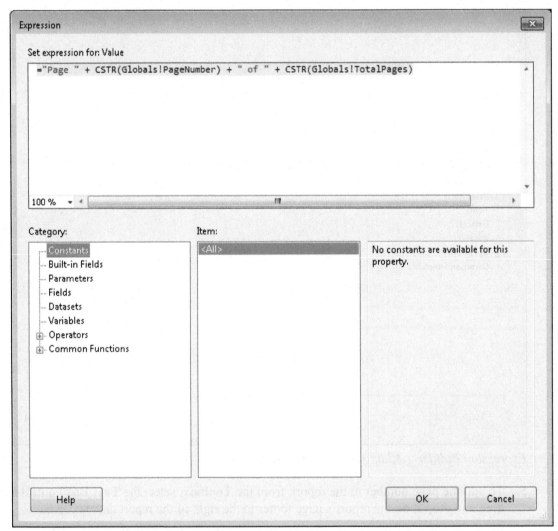

Expression Builder—Adding page numbers.

7. Click **Preview** to view the custom report date and page numbers.

Note: You may receive a warning regarding formatting of the page number. You can safely ignore that warning as it will not affect the report. Optionally, as shown in the following figure, you can expand the width of the txtReportDate and txtPageNumber fields.

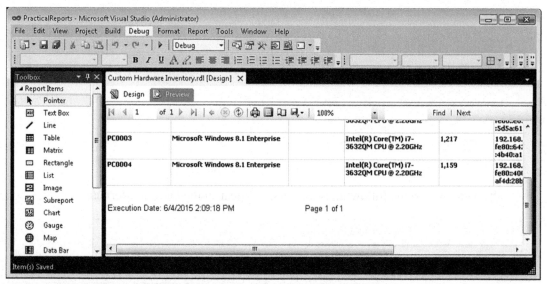

Report Preview view with the report date and page number.

Deploy the Completed Report

In a previous exercise, you deployed the entire PracticalReports reporting solution to SSRS. There are times when all you'll need to do is deploy a single report.

To deploy your finalized Custom Hardware Inventory report to SSRS, take the following steps:

1. In the SQL Server Data Tools – PracticalReports solution, browse to the **Solution Explorer**.

2. Select the **Custom Hardware Inventory.rdl** report, right-click, and then click **Deploy**.

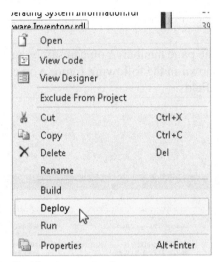

Deploying a single report.

You should see the following information appear in the Output interface:

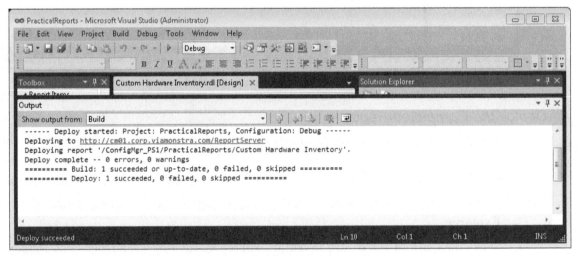

SQL Server Data Tools—Deploying a single report.

Simplifying Report Data

One of the more challenging aspects of creating custom reports is deciding which data elements to display and how much data to display. No user wants to navigate potentially thousands of records of results to locate the data that they need!

There are several approaches to simplifying report data. The following concepts are explored: in this section:

- Report grouping
- Report parameters
- Linked reports

Report Grouping

Report grouping allows one or more data fields to be organized to consolidate report data. Grouping can be used to create stepped reports, or reports that can be expanded by clicking on grouped fields. Examples of report grouping may include displaying computers organized by site, operating system, hardware type, and so forth.

In this section, you create a new report that groups computers by operating system and then by service pack.

You have been asked to provide the following information in this custom operating system report:

- Operating system name
- Service pack name
- Computer name
- Total memory (MB)

Complete the following steps to create a report that groups computers by operating system and then by service pack:

1. If the **SQL Server Data Tools** development environment is not already open, perform these steps to start it:

    a. On **PC0001**, log on as **VIAMONSTRA\Administrator**.

    b. Start **SQL Server Data Tools**, and from the **Start Page**, click **Open Project**. Double-click the **PracticalReports** folder, select the solution file **PracticalReports.sln**, and click **Open**.

2. In the **Solution Explorer**, right-click **Reports**, and then click **Add New Report**.

> **Note**: If the Solution Explorer is not open, from the menu bar, click View / Solution Explorer.

3. On the **Welcome to the Report Wizard** page, click **Next**. Allow **Shared data source** to default to **CMPS1**. Click **Next**.

4. On the **Design the Query** page, type the following query into the into the **Query string** window (you also can copy and paste from the Chapter7/Ch7-2 Grouping.sql file in the book sample files). Click **Next**.

```
SELECT s.ResourceID,
    s.Netbios_Name0 AS ComputerName,
    os.Caption0 AS OperatingSystemName,
    os.CSDVersion0 AS ServicePack,
    m.TotalPhysicalMemory0 / 1024 AS TotalMemoryMB
FROM v_R_System_Valid s
INNER JOIN v_GS_OPERATING_SYSTEM os
    ON s.ResourceID = os.ResourceID
INNER JOIN v_GS_COMPUTER_SYSTEM gs
    ON s.ResourceID = gs.ResourceID
INNER JOIN v_GS_X86_PC_MEMORY m
    ON s.ResourceID = m.ResourceID
```

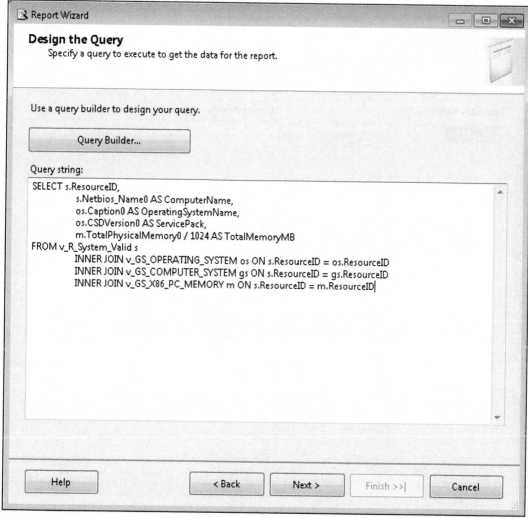

Report Wizard—Design the Query.

5. On the **Select the Report Type** page, set the report type to **Tabular** and click **Next**.

6. On the **Design the Table** page, add the available fields in this order:

    a. Select **OperatingSystemName**, and then click **Group**.

    b. Select **ServicePack**, and then click **Group**.

    c. Select **ComputerName**, and then click **Details**.

    d. Select **TotalMemoryMB**, and then click **Details**.

    e. Click **Next**.

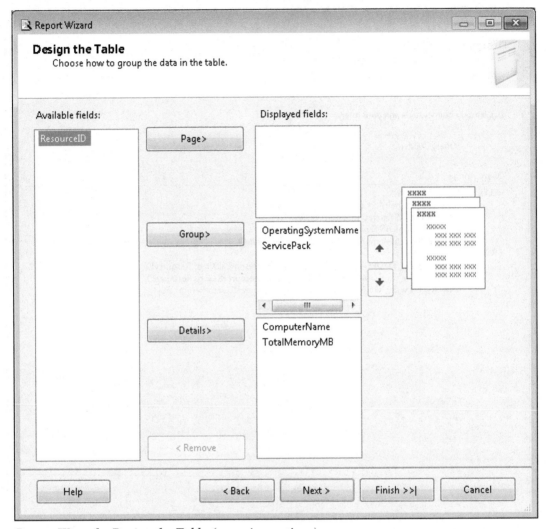

Report Wizard—Design the Table (grouping options).

7.   On the **Choose the Table Layout** page, perform the following:

   a.   Select **Stepped**.

   b.   Select **Enable Drilldown**.

   c.   Click **Next**.

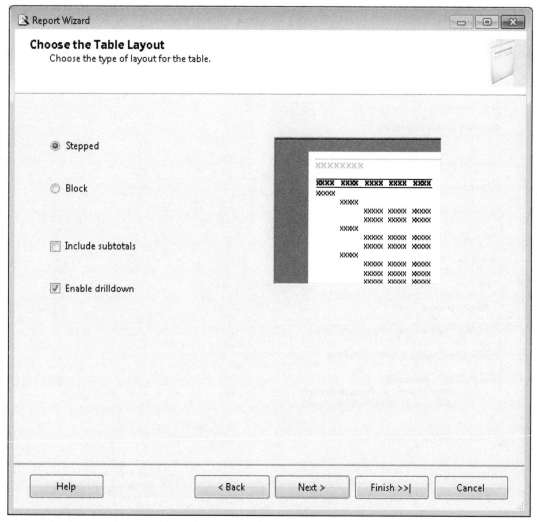

Report Wizard—Choose the Table Layout (grouping options).

Note: The Enable drilldown option collapses the report data by group, allowing the report user to click and expand the elements for which they want to see more detail.

8. On the **Choose the Table Style** page, accept the default settings and click **Next**.

9. On the **Completing the Wizard** page, name the report **Operating System Summary**, enable the **Preview report** option (lower left), and then click **Finish**.

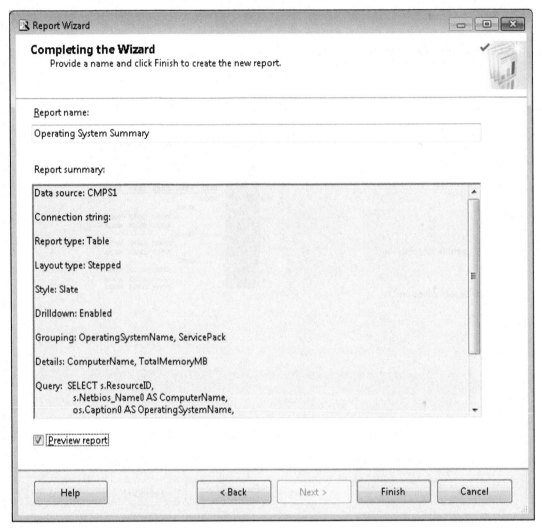

Report Wizard—Completing the Wizard.

10. The report should appear in Preview view. Click to expand the **Operating System Name** and **Service Pack** information columns to display the computer information.

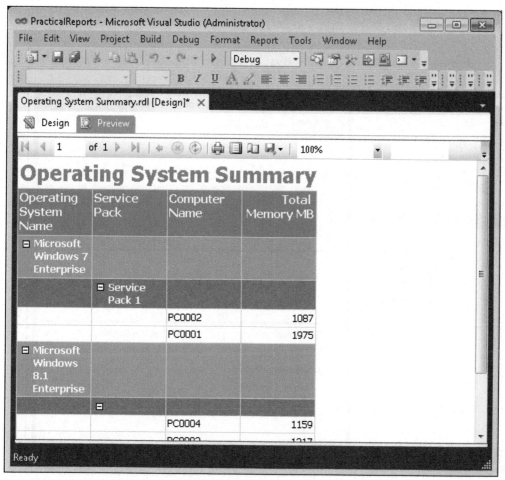

Operating System Summary with grouping.

Real World Note: This approach to grouping data with drilldown capability is a very handy way to display complex data in a concise way. You do notice where there is no service pack (after Windows 8.1 Enterprise), there is a blank, or more accurately, a NULL data element being returned. It is often the case with the Report Wizard, however, that the reports need some refinement. You solve this next.

In order to correct the missing service pack name, you take the following steps:

1. For the **Operating System Name** report, click **Design**.

2. Select **View / Report Data**. Expand the **Datasets** node, and then expand the **DataSet1** dataset.

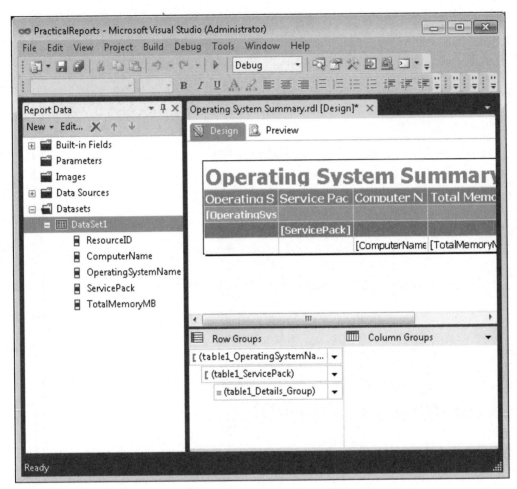

Operating System Summary—Datasets.

Note: The fields displayed are the dataset elements returned and available to the report. However, you need to edit the actual dataset query to modify the SQL statement.

---

3. Right-click **DataSet1**, and then click **Dataset Properties**. Perform the following tasks:

   a. In the query, locate the **ServicePack** field: **os.CSDVersion0 AS ServicePack**.

   b. Replace that line with: **ISNULL(os.CSDVersion0, 'None') AS ServicePack**.

Note: This will replace any NULL values with our substitution "None".

---

   c. To test this change, click **Query Designer**, and then click the **Execution** button (!) to run the query.

Note: You should see that the substitution for the missing service pack entry is working.

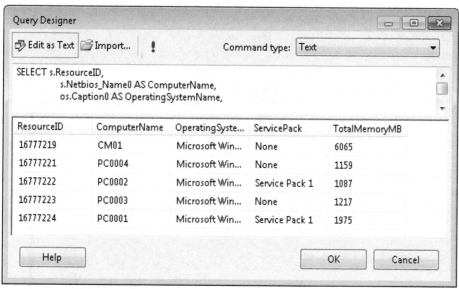

Query Designer results.

4. Click **OK**, and then click **OK** again to close the **DataSet1 Properties**.

5. Click **Preview**, and for the **Operating System Name** column, click and expand **Windows 8.1**. Then expand **Service Pack**.

Note: With the Operating System Name column expanded, note that the Service Pack field has a valid substitution of None.

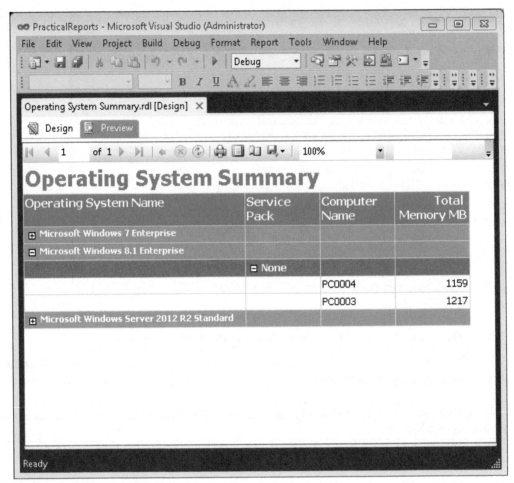

Operating System Summary—Service pack name substitution.

Report Parameters

Report parameters allow the user of the report to be prompted to select one or more parameters. After they are selected, the report is generated based on those parameters.

There are several advantages of parameters:

- They are usually derived from data that will be in the reports.

- They act as report filters, limiting the amount of information being returned.

- More than one parameter can be used, each limited by the preceding one. These are known as *cascading parameters*.

In this section, you create a report using a parameter to return computers by a specific operating system.

You have been asked to provide the following information in this custom operating system report:

- Operating system name
- Service pack name
- Computer name
- Computer model
- Processor type speed
- Total memory (MB)
- Last boot-up time

Complete the following steps to create a report using a parameter to return computers by a specific operating system:

1. If the **SQL Server Data Tools** development environment is not already open, perform these steps to start it:

    a. On **PC0001**, log on as **VIAMONSTRA\Administrator**.

    b. Start **SQL Server Data Tools**, and from the **Start Page**, click **Open Project**. Double-click the **PracticalReports** folder, select the solution file **PracticalReports.sln**, and click **Open**.

2. In the **Solution Explorer**, right-click **Reports**, and then click **Add New Report**.

3. On the **Welcome to the Report Wizard** page, click **Next**.

4. On the **Select the Data Source** page, allow **Shared data source** to default to **CMPS1**. Click **Next**.

5. On the **Design the Query** page, type the following query in the **Query string** window (you also can copy and paste from the Chapter7/Ch7-3 Parameters.sql file in the book sample files). Click **Next**.

```
SELECT s.ResourceID,
    os.Caption0 AS OperatingSystemName,
    ISNULL(os.CSDVersion0, 'None') AS ServicePack,
    s.Netbios_Name0 AS ComputerName,
    gs.Model0 AS ComputerModel,
    p.Name0 AS ProcessorName,
    m.TotalPhysicalMemory0 / 1024 AS TotalMemoryMB,
    os.LastBootUpTime0 as LastBootUpTime
FROM v_R_System_Valid s
```

```
    INNER JOIN v_GS_OPERATING_SYSTEM os ON s.ResourceID =
os.ResourceID

    INNER JOIN v_GS_COMPUTER_SYSTEM gs ON s.ResourceID =
gs.ResourceID

    INNER JOIN v_GS_X86_PC_MEMORY m ON s.ResourceID =
m.ResourceID

    INNER JOIN v_GS_PROCESSOR p ON s.ResourceID =
p.ResourceID
```

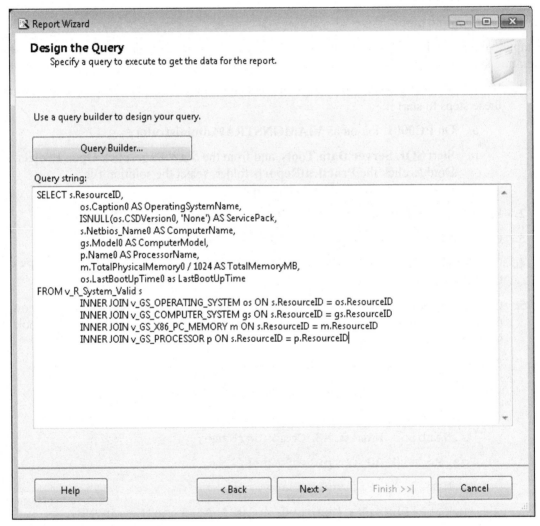

Report Wizard—Design the Query.

6. On the **Select the Report Type** page, set the report type to **Tabular** and click **Next**.

7. On the **Design the Table** page, add the available fields in this order:

    a. Select **OperatingSystemName**, and then click **Details**.

    b. Select **ServicePack**, and then click **Details**.

    c. Select **ComputerName**, and then click **Details**.

    d. Select **ComputerModel**, and then click **Details**.

    e. Select **ProcessorName**, and then click **Details**.

    f. Select **TotalMemoryMB**, and then click **Details**.

    g. Select **LastBootUpTime**, and then click **Details**.

    h. Click **Next**.

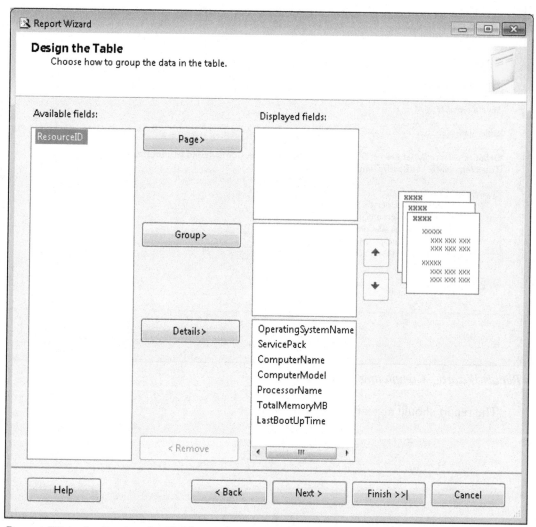

Report Wizard—Design the Table (grouping options).

8. On the **Choose the Table Style** page, accept the default and click **Next**.

9. On the **Completing the Wizard** page, name the report **Operating System with Parameter**, enable the **Preview report** option (lower left), and then click **Finish**.

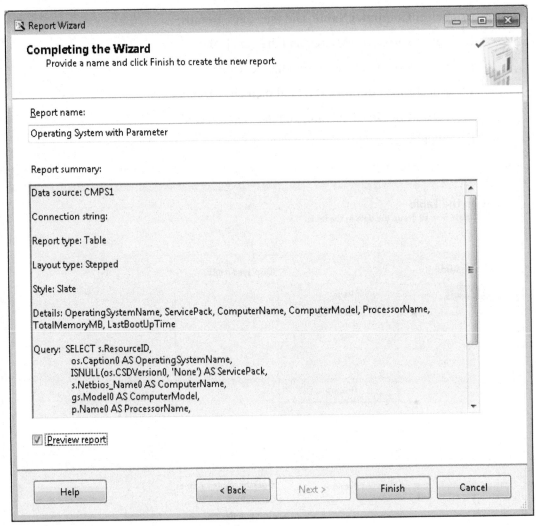

Report Wizard—Completing the Wizard.

The report should appear in Preview view.

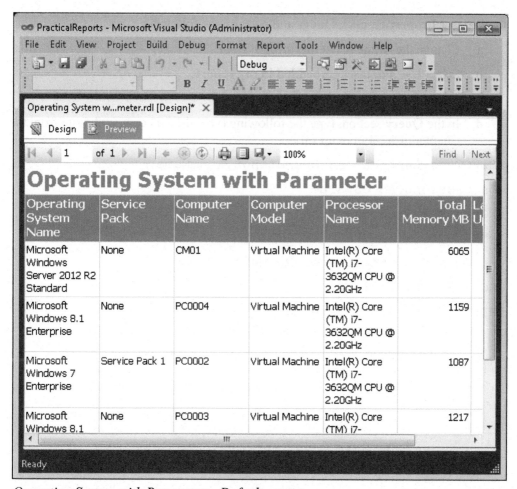

Operating System with Parameter—Default report.

Now, you need to make a few report modifications and then add a parameter. The sequence for adding a query, or data-driven parameter to a report is as follows:

1.   Create a new dataset.

2.   Create a new parameter.

3.   Modify the report query to use the parameter.

Create a New Dataset

1.   Toggle the report to **Design** view.

2.   Select the **report title** and change it to **Operating System Lookup**.

3.   From the menu bar, click **View / Report Data**.

4.   Click **Datasets**, right-click, and click **Add Datasets**.

5. On **Dataset Properties**, click **Query** and perform the following:

    a. Change the **Name** to **dsOperatingSystem**.

    b. Select **Use a dataset embedded in my report**.

    c. Under **Data source**: select **CMPS1**

    d. In the **Query** section, type the following (you also can copy and paste from the Chapter7/Ch7-4 Lookup.sql).

```
SELECT os.Caption0 AS OperatingSystemName,
 os.Caption0 AS OSValue
FROM v_R_System_Valid s
INNER JOIN v_GS_OPERATING_SYSTEM os
    ON s.ResourceID = os.ResourceID
GROUP BY os.Caption0
ORDER BY OperatingSystemName
```

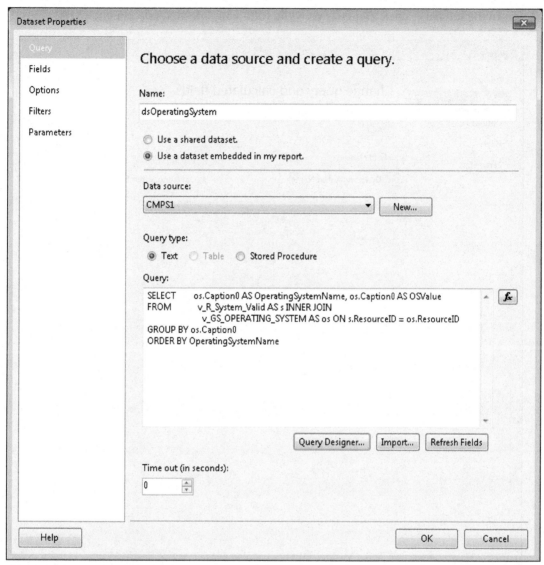

Dataset Properties—Query.

Note: You may notice that you are repeating the OS Caption field (os.Caption0) in this query. This is by design. Report parameters require a caption that is displayed to the user and a value that is used internally by reporting services.

6. In the left pane, click **Fields**, review the following information, and click **OK**.

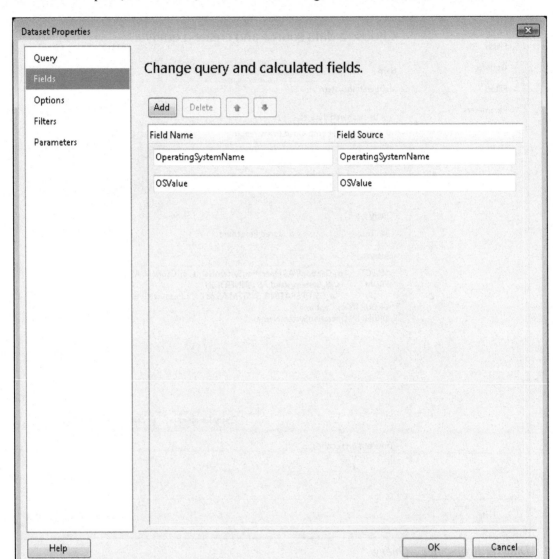

Dataset Properties—Fields.

Create a New Parameter

1. From the menu bar, select **View** / **Report Data** (click somewhere in the report first if not available in the menu).

2. Click **Parameters**, right-click, and click **Add Parameter**.

3. On **Report Parameter Properties**, click **General** and perform the following:

    a. Change the **Name** to **prmOperatingSystem**.

    b. Change the **Prompt** to **Select Operating System**.

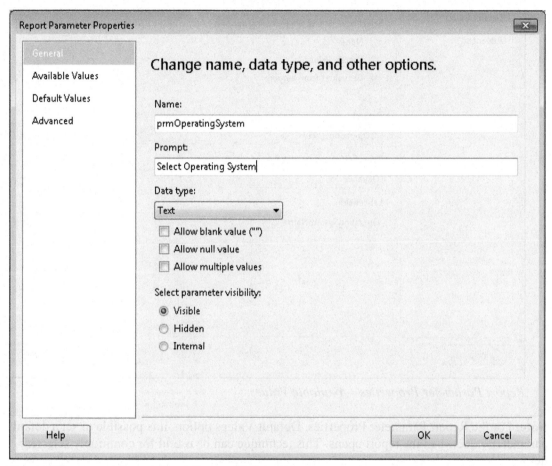

Report Parameter Properties—General information.

4. In the left pane, click **Available Values**, and perform the following:

    a. Under **Select from the one of the following options**, select the **Get Values from a Query** option.

    b. Under **Dataset**, select **dsOperatingSystem**.

    c. Under **Value Field**, select **OSValue**.

    d. Under **Label Field**, select **OperatingSystemName**.

    e. Click **OK**.

145

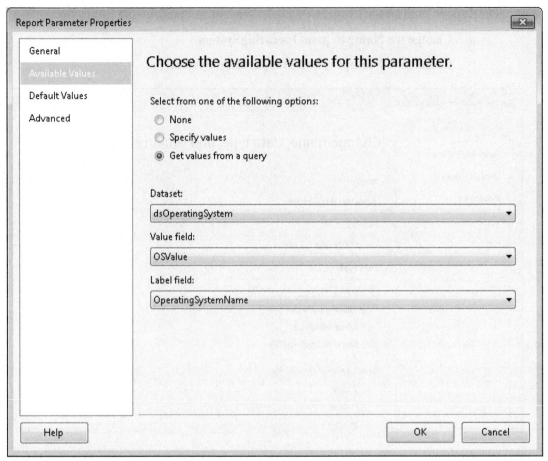

Report Parameter Properties—Available Values.

Note: For the Report Parameter Properties, Default Values option, it is possible to set a default parameter value when the report opens. This technique can be useful for commonly selected items.

Modify the Report Query to Use the Parameter

1. In **Report Data**, click and expand **Datasets**.
2. Select and right-click **Dataset1**, and choose **Dataset Properties**.
3. Click **Query**, type the following line at the end of the existing query, and click **OK**:

```
WHERE os.Caption0 LIKE @prmOperatingSystem
```

Note: The name of the parameter created is used in the query. Internally, the Value field is used by the query to locate a matching condition.

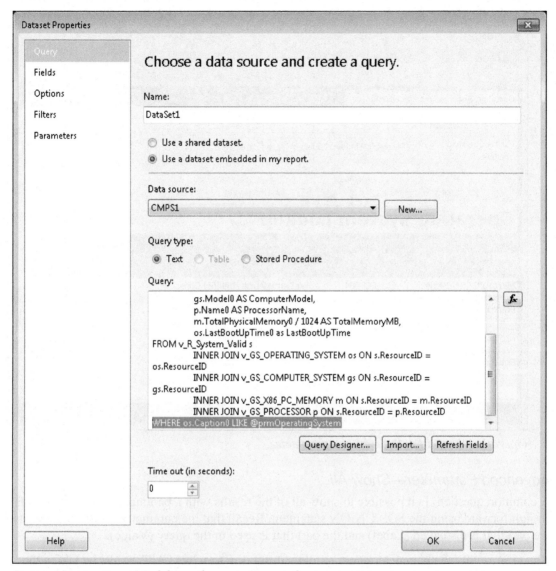

Dataset Properties—Modifying the query to use the parameter.

4. Click **Preview** to test. In the report parameter, select **Microsoft Windows 8.1 Enterprise** and then click **View Report**.

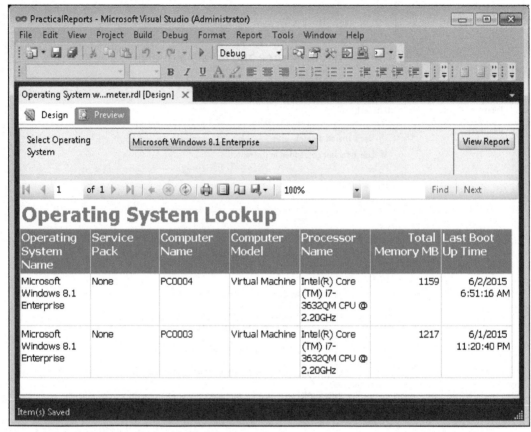

Operating System Lookup with the parameter.

Advanced Parameter—Show All

A common question: Is it possible to show all of the results with a parameter selection? It is fairly straightforward using the SQL UNION statement. Recall that the parameter uses two elements: the part that is displayed (Label) and the part that is used in the query (Value).

You now modify the parameter query to allow the ability to select "All" results by taking the following steps:

1. Toggle the report to **Design** view.

2. From the menu bar, select **View / Report Data**.

3. Click **Datasets**, right-click **dsOperatingSystem**, and select **Dataset Properties**.

4. In **Dataset Properties**, click **Query**. In the **Query** section, replace the existing query by typing the following (you also can copy and paste from the Chapter7/Ch7-5 Advanced Parameters.sql) and clicking **OK**:

```
SELECT '<All>' AS OperatingSystemName,
  '%' AS OSValue
UNION
SELECT
  os.Caption0 AS OperatingSystemName,
  os.Caption0 AS OSValue
FROM v_R_System_Valid s
INNER JOIN v_GS_OPERATING_SYSTEM os
    ON s.ResourceID = os.ResourceID
GROUP BY os.Caption0
```

> **Real World Note**: What the UNION statement does, is take advantage of using the Label to display <All>, and the Value to substitute the wildcard percent symbol (%). The underlying report query uses this information in the WHERE criteria. When the parameter query is used with the LIKE operator, the percent (%) symbol causes the SQL statement to return all rows.

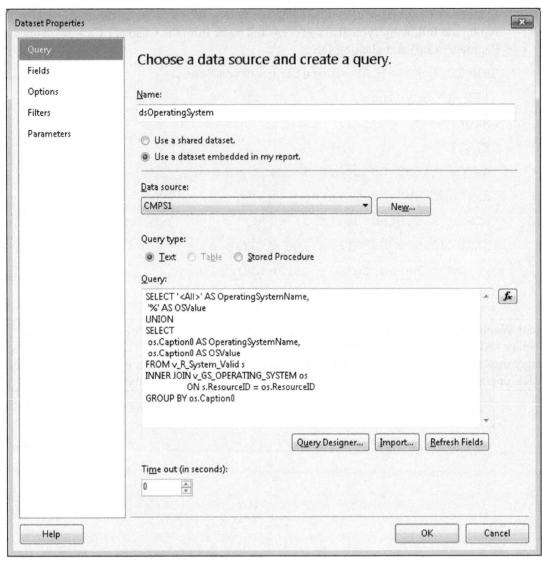

Dataset Properties—Modifying the query.

5. Click **Preview** to test. In the report parameter, select **<All>**, and then click **View Report**.

Note: All of the rows are returned, and the other operating system parameters will continue to function properly.

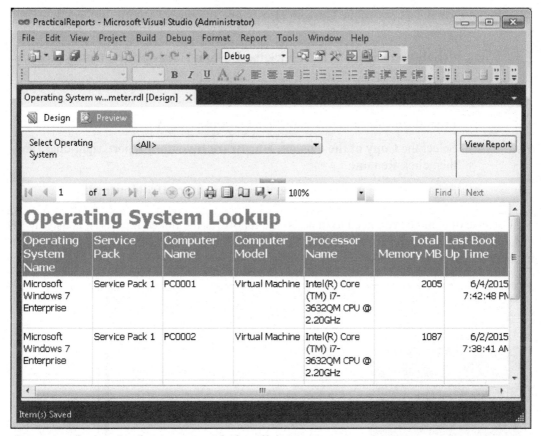

Operating System Lookup report with the All parameter.

Linked Reports

Linked reports are reports that are invoked, or linked from other reports. This is another technique to direct the report user from summary-level data to more detail-level data. It is entirely possible to have more than two linked reports.

Linked reports are passed variables from the parent report to the child report, with the child report returning a subset of information based on those variable(s).

In this section, using two reports that you have previously created, you use a summary-level report and link this report to the Custom Hardware Inventory report created earlier in this chapter. Complete the following steps to create the linked report:

1. If the **SQL Server Data Tools** development environment is not already open, perform these steps to start it:

    a. On **PC0001**, log on as **VIAMONSTRA\Administrator**.

    b. Start **SQL Server Data Tools**, and from the **Start Page**, click **Open Project**. Double-click the **PracticalReports** folder, select the solution file **PracticalReports.sln**, and click **Open**.

2. You now make a copy of the **Custom Hardware Inventory** report. Perform the following steps:

   a. In **Solution Explorer**, right-click the **Custom Hardware Inventory** report and then click **Copy**.

   b. In the **Solution Explorer**, select the **Reports** node.

   c. From the menu bar, click **Edit / Paste** (or use Ctrl+V).

   d. Select the **Copy of the Custom Hardware Inventory** report, right-click, and then click **Rename**.

   e. Rename the report **Custom Hardware Inventory Drilldown.rdl**.

> **Note**: Because of changes you need to make to the report for the linked reports, it is usually better to make a report copy of the child report. Additionally, making copies of reports is often useful as a starting point for report enhancements.

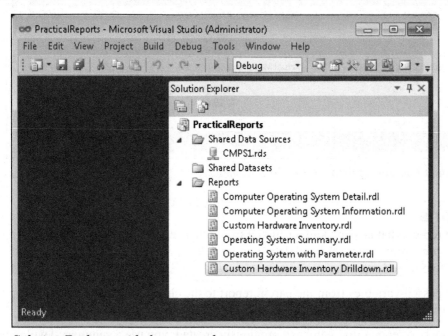

Solution Explorer with the renamed report copy.

3. In **Solution Explorer**, double-click the **Custom Hardware Inventory Drilldown** report to open it in. If it does not open in Design view, click **Design** to change the view.

4. From the menu bar, select **View / Report Data**.

5. In **Report Data**, right-click **Parameters** and then click **Add Parameter**.

6. In the **Report Parameter Properties** window, take the following actions:

    a. For **Name**, type **prmResourceID**.

    b. For **Prompt**, type **prmResourceID**.

    c. For **Data type**, select **Integer**.

    d. Enable **Allow null value**.

    e. For **Select parameter visibility**, select **Hidden**.

    f. Click **OK**.

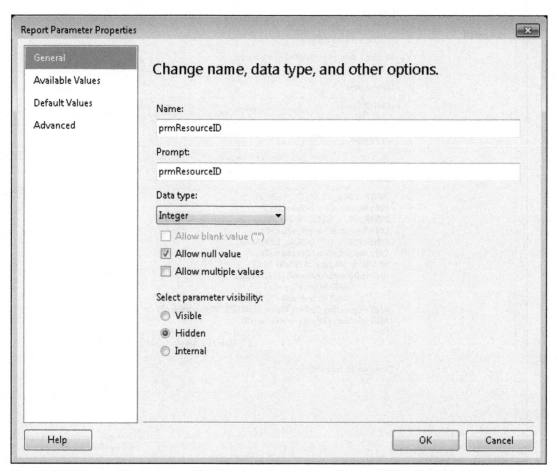

Report Parameter Properties—Configuring the report parameter for a linked report.

7. In **Report Data**, click and expand the **Datasets** node. Right-click **DataSet1**, and then click **Dataset Properties**.

8. In **Dataset Properties**, click **Query** option, add the following line to the end of the query statement, and then click **OK**:

```
AND s.ResourceID = @prmResourceID
```

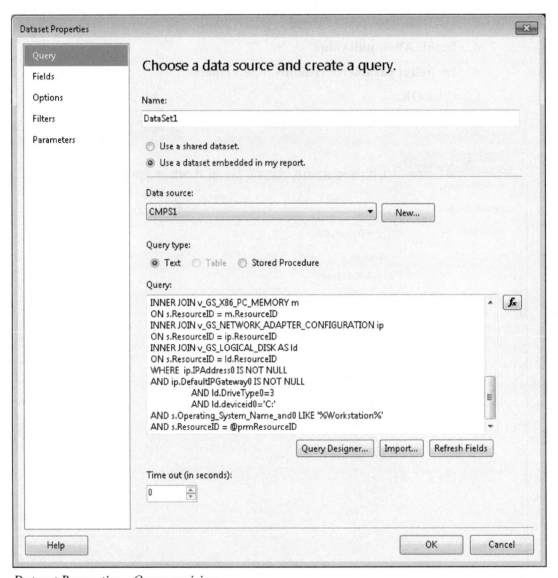

Dataset Properties—Query revision.

Note: If the Define Query Properties dialog box appears, click OK.

9. Save the changes to the **Custom Hardware Inventory Drilldown** report.

10. In **Solution Explorer**, double-click the **Operating System Summary** report, to open in **Design** view. If it does not open in Design view, click **Design** to change the view.

11. Select the data cell for **[ComputerName]**, right-click, and select **Text Box Properties**.

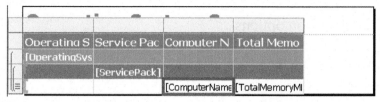

The [ComputerName] data cell selected in Design view.

12. In the **Text Box Properties** window, perform the following actions:

    a.   In the left pane, click **Action**.

    b.   For **Enable as an action**, choose **Go to report**.

    c.   For **Specify a report**, select **Custom Hardware Inventory Drilldown**.

    d.   For **Use these parameters to run the report**, click **Add**.

    e.   For **Name**, select **prmResourceID**.

    f.   For **Value**, select **[ResourceID]**.

    g.   Click **OK**.

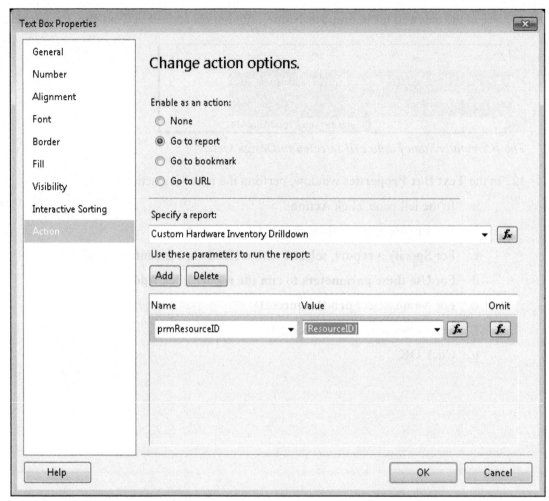

Text Box Properties—Action page.

Note: The Action property allows you to create the link to another child report. Further, you need to pass a parameter or data from the current row to the linked report to allow the child report to filter information based on that passed parameter. Additionally, as needed, it may be necessary to pass more than one parameter depending on circumstances.

13. Select the data cell for **[ComputerName]**. On the toolbar, select font **Bold**, font **Underline**, and font **Foreground Color (Blue).**

> **Note:** If you did not take these actions, a hyperlink would exist and report users would not know that it was there!

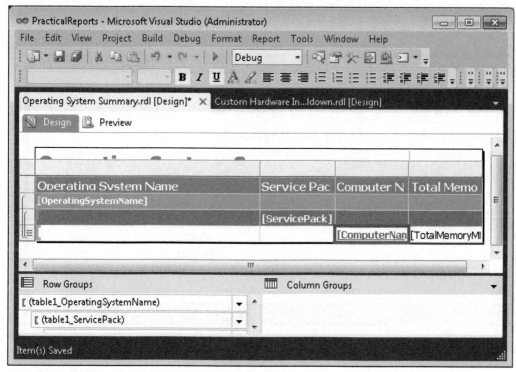

Report Design—Computer Name revision.

14. To test these revisions, for the **Computer Operating System Summary** report, select **Preview**. Expand one of the **Operating System Name** entries, expand the **Service Pack** name, and then click the value for **Computer Name**.

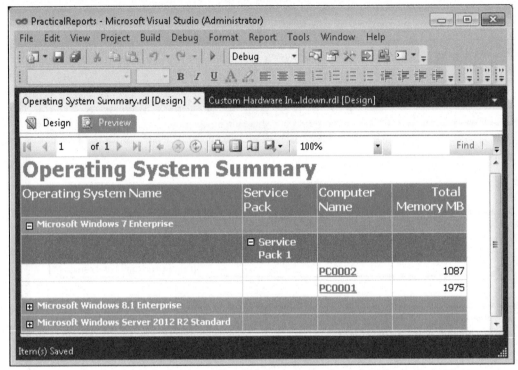

Operating System Summary report with a linked field.

It should load the linked Custom Hardware Inventory report, with the detail for the Computer Name value that was clicked. Results for PC0001 follow:

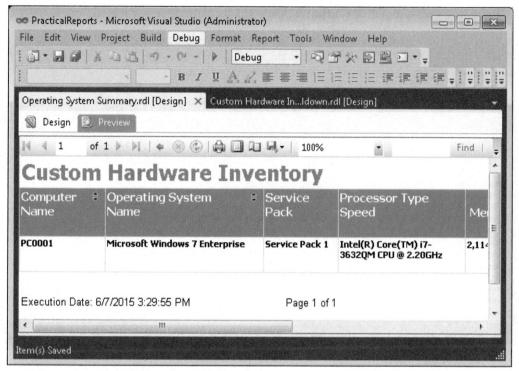

The Custom Hardware Inventory linked report.

Deploy All Completed Reports

To ensure that all new reports and enhanced reports are deployed to SSRS, you now deploy the PracticalReports solution.

To deploy your finalized Custom Hardware Inventory report to SSRS, take the following steps:

1.   In the **SQL Server Data Tools**, **PracticalReports** solution, select **Build / Deploy PracticalReports**.

Deploying the solution.

2. Review the representative **Output** window for success, or any potential issues.

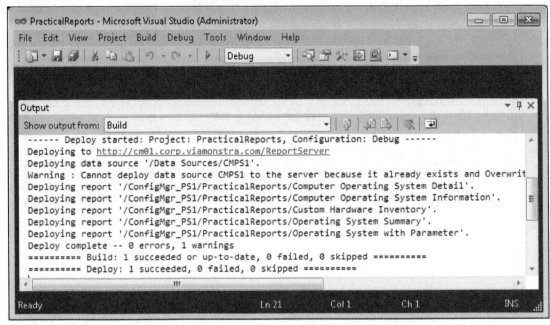

SQL Server Data Tools—Output.

3. Test the reports and report parameters on SSRS.

Summary

In this chapter, you have learned how to extend hardware inventory, create custom reports, and explore interactive report features. You have demonstrated various techniques for simplifying the display of report data.

The methods investigated for displaying report data; included report grouping, report parameters, and linked reports. Occasionally, reports can and will use a combination of these techniques to assist the user in navigating the information. Make use of the interactive report features to allow a better experience when viewing report data.

Which method should be used for report creation depends on the end-user objective. Take the time to design the report data display and the report flow, typically from summary level to more detailed report view. Working on the report flow and design prior to creating the actual reports often saves development time!

Resources

The following resources are useful articles from Microsoft and other community sources as appropriate:

Expression Examples (Report Builder and SSRS)
https://msdn.microsoft.com/en-us/library/ms157328.aspx

Report Parameters (Report Builder and Report Designer)
https://msdn.microsoft.com/en-us/library/dd220464(v=sql.130).aspx

Chapter 8

Reporting on Other Databases

Reporting on databases other than Configuration Manager is fairly common. In this practical reporting chapter, you learn how track Configuration Manager clients as they are both added to *and removed from* the Configuration Manager database. This valuable information is captured daily, and reports are created exposing this data.

Step-by-Step Guide Requirements

If you want to follow the step-by-step guides in this chapter, you need a lab environment configured as outlined in Chapter 1, have configured Reporting Services in Chapter 2, and have installed SQL Server Management Studio on PC0001 in Chapter 3. In this chapter, you use the following virtual machines:

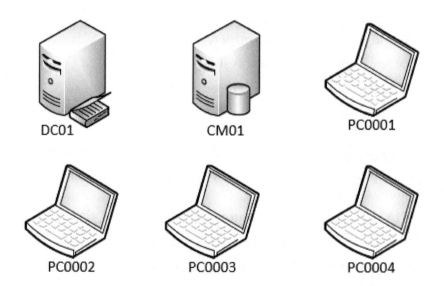

The VMs used in this chapter.

You should have the following software installed on PC0001:

- Configuration Manager 2012 Console

- Configuration Manager 2012 Console Cumulative Update Hotfix

163

- SQL Server Management Studio

- SQL Server Data Tools

Note: If you have not installed SQL Server Management Studio on PC0001, please review the setup process in Chapter 3. Additionally, you need to set up SQL Server Data Tools for first use, as described in the beginning of Chapter 6.

How to Retain Inventory Information

You have been asked to capture and retain computer information inventoried by Configuration Manager. Normally, when the Configuration Manager maintenance tasks run, clients that no longer report inventory are deleted from the Configuration Manager database.

Because best practice dictates that no table objects are added to the Configuration Manager database, the easiest way to solve this issue is to create a custom database. Within the custom database, you can track the computers being added to and removed from Configuration Manager.

This task is handled in the following order:

1. Creating the custom database named CMMonitor

2. Optionally, implementing the index and statistics optimization process

3. Adding the required table to support the data-retention request

4. Adding the stored procedure to capture the inventory data

5. Adding an SQL Server Agent task to run the stored procedure daily

6. Importing the custom inventory reports

Create the Custom Database

In this guide, I assume you have copied the book sample files to C:\Setup on CM01. Complete the following steps to create the custom database:

1. On **CM01**, log on as **VIAMONSTRA\Administrator**.

2. Start and run the **SQL Server Management Studio** (SSMS) console.

3. When prompted for connection, enter **CM01** for the database name and connect using **Windows Authentication**. Click **OK**.

4. Open an elevated **PowerShell** prompt, and create the new, custom database named **CMMonitor** by running the following command (the command is wrapped and should be one line):

```
Invoke-Sqlcmd -QueryTimeout 0
-InputFile C:\Setup\Chapter8\1-CreateCMMonitorDB.sql
```

> **Note:** Again, setting QueryTimeout to 0 means no timeout. The default timeout (30 seconds) is often not enough to create the databases, especially if the disk subsystem is slow.

5. On the left side of the **SSMS console**, click the **Databases** node to expand Databases and verify that the **CMMonitor** database is present.

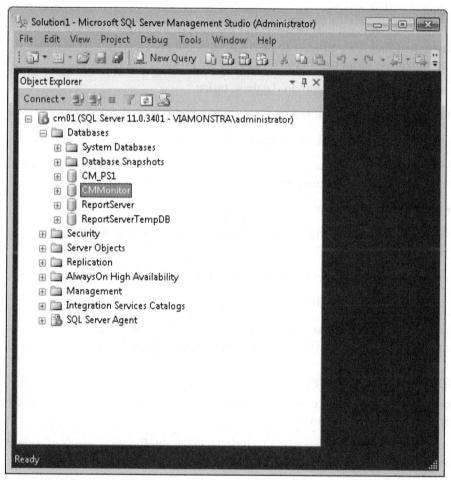

The CMMonitor database.

> **Note**: For this chapter, up to the "Import the Custom Reports" section, you work from the CM01 console. Leave the SSMS interface open and leave the elevated PowerShell interface active.

Implementing the Index and Statistics Optimization Process

While not directly related to Reporting Services, implementing a tuning solution helps your reports run faster! Out-of-date database statistics and indexes *will* slow almost any database operation that involves reading, inserting, deleting, or updating records. Currently, the best solution for this issue is an open-source database index and statistics optimization script that can be scheduled to run on a regular basis.

Authored by Ola Hallengren, it is used by many major companies including Dell and Microsoft. I have observed queries that took 10+ minutes to return results, but provided results in under 10 seconds after the optimization script had been run against the problematic database.

Ola Hallengren's scripts covers most common database tasks:

- Full, Differential, or Transaction log backups of user and system databases

- Integration with third-party backup solutions

- Dynamic index optimization that reorganizes, rebuilds, or ignores indexes based on the amount of fragmentation or page count.

- Online or offline rebuild options use determination.

- Database integrity checks that check entire databases (DBCC CHECKDB) or more granular portions

- Maintenance clean up task to delete backup and job history and clean up logs

- Log events to maintenance database

- Option to create all the maintenance jobs automatically by running the MaintenanceSolution.sql script (schedule the required jobs to run)

Implement Index Optimization Scripts

These highly recommended, open-source scripts are created by Ola Hallengren. They are used by Microsoft, Dell, and many other companies.

These scripts allow a very granular optimization technique, using intelligent rebuilds of indexes based on fragmentation and updating of statistics as needed.

On the SQL Server instance that needs to be optimized, a default implementation follows:

1. On **CM01**, open an elevated **PowerShell** prompt, and create the new, custom database named **CMMonitor** by running the following command (the command is wrapped and should be one line):

```
Invoke-Sqlcmd -QueryTimeout 0 -InputFile C:\Setup\
Chapter8\2-MaintenanceSolution.sql
```

> **Note**: The preceding script was downloaded and modified for this book. The details for the modifications for this script are as follows:
>
> 1. From http://ola.hallengren.com/sql-server-index-and-statistics-maintenance.html, download the MaintenanceSolution.sql script to a local source folder.
>
> 2. Using a text editor, open the script; then using find and replace (on the first page), change USE [MASTER] to USE [CMMONITOR].

2. In the **SSMS console**, browse to and expand the **CMMonitor** database node; then click to expand the **Tables** node and the **Stored Procedures** node. The follow table and stored procedure objects should be present:

- CMMonitor
    - Database Diagrams
    - Tables
        - System Tables
        - FileTables
        - dbo.CommandLog
    - Views
    - Synonyms
    - Programmability
        - Stored Procedures
            - System Stored Procedures
            - dbo.CommandExecute
            - dbo.DatabaseBackup
            - dbo.DatabaseIntegrityCheck
            - dbo.IndexOptimize

Database objects required for optimization.

As the final task in this solution, enable the scheduling of the SQL Server Agent tasks. To take this action, perform the following steps.

3. In the **SSMS console**, browse to and select the **SQL Server Agent** node. If it is not running, right-click **SQL Server Agent** and then click **Start**.

4. Click to expand the **SQL Server Agent** node, and then click to expand **Jobs**. You should have a list that is similar to this one:

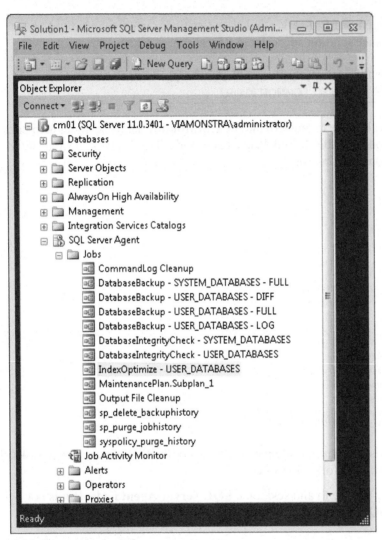

SQL Server Agent Jobs.

5. In the **SQL Server Agent / Jobs** node, right-click **CommandLog Cleanup**, and then click **Properties**.

6. In the left pane, select **Schedule**, and then click **New**.

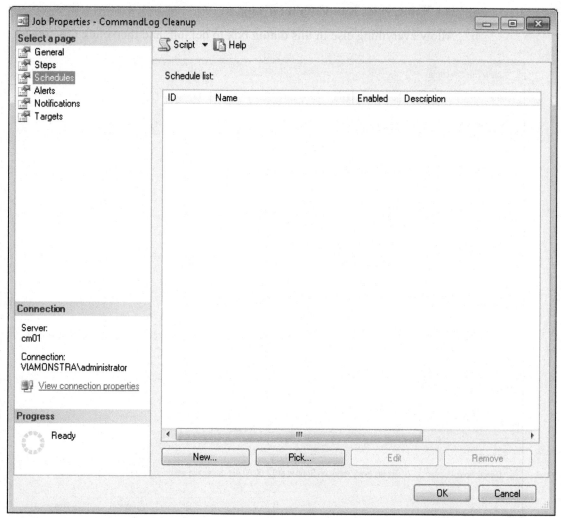

Job Properties—Schedules.

7. Perform the following steps:

   a. For **Name**, enter **Run CommandLog**.

   b. Allow everything else in this dialog box to default, and then click **OK** twice.

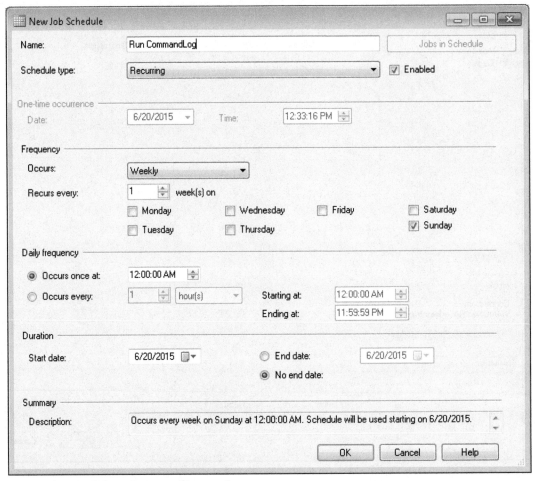

New Job Schedule—CommandLog task.

Note: The CommandLog purges records older than 30 days from the CommandLog table. As such, this needs to run only one time per week.

Now, you need to schedule the Index and Statistic optimization task for the databases. You take the following steps:

8. In the **SQL Server Agent / Jobs** node, right-click **IndexOptimize - USER_DATABASES**, and then click **Properties**.

9. In the left pane, select **Schedule**, and then click **New**.

10. Perform the following steps:

    a. For **Name**, enter **Run Optimize**.

    b. For **Frequency**, enable **Wednesday** and **Sunday**.

    c. For **Daily frequency**, change occurs once at **01:00AM**.

    d. Then click **OK**.

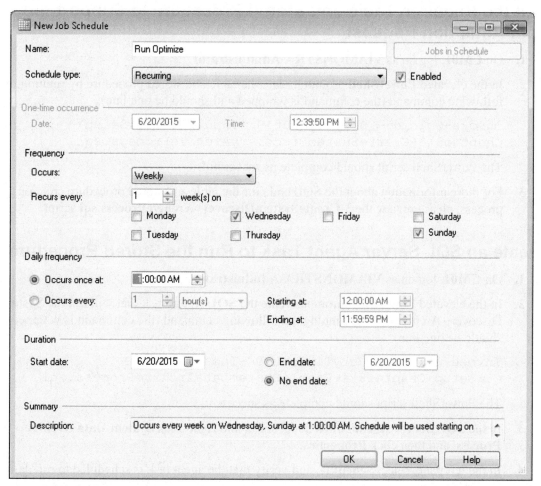

New Job Schedule—Run Optimize task.

Note: The Run Optimize task is scheduled to run two times per week. If required, the task can be run more frequently. The more frequently it is run, the less index and statistic optimization that needs to be accomplished.

11. Click **OK** to save changes.

Implementation Notes

Large, heavily fragmented databases may take a long time to complete. Plan to run after hours and during low user activity.

When run on databases with Full recovery mode set, be aware that there needs to be sufficient free log space available. It is possible to customize the index optimization process.

Add the Required Table and Stored Procedure to Support the Data-Retention Request

1. On **CM01**, log on as **VIAMONSTRA\Administrator**.

2. In the elevated **PowerShell** prompt, create the table and stored procedure by running the following command (the command is wrapped and should be one line):

    ```
    Invoke-Sqlcmd -QueryTimeout 0 -InputFile C:\Setup\
    Chapter8\3-CreateSystemDiscoveryArchiveProcess.sql
    ```

    The PowerShell script should complete as successful.

3. For more information about the SQL code for the table and stored procedure creation process, please review the **3-CreateSystemDiscoveryArchiveProcess.sql** script.

Create an SQL Server Agent Task to Run the Stored Procedure

1. On **CM01**, log on as **VIAMONSTRA\Administrator**.

2. In the elevated **PowerShell** prompt, create the **SQL Agent** task that will run the System Discovery Archive task by running the following command (the command is wrapped and should be one line):

    ```
    Invoke-Sqlcmd -QueryTimeout 0 -InputFile
    C:\Setup\Chapter8\4-EnableSystemDataArchiveProcess.sql
    ```

    The PowerShell script should complete as successful.

3. In the **SQL Server Agent / Jobs** node, select and right-click **System Data Archive Process**, and then click **Properties**.

4. In the left pane, select **Schedule**, and verify that the agent task is scheduled to run daily at 5:00 AM. Click **Cancel** to close.

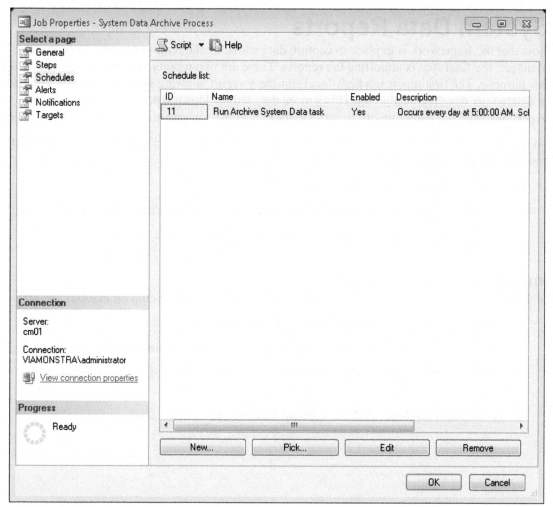

Job Properties—System Data Archive Process.

Note: Once a day at 5:00AM, this process runs as two steps. It first inserts any new Configuration Manager system data into the CMMonitor custom table SystemDiscoveryArchive. Any data added during this process sets a custom InsertedDate field with the current date. The second step performs a reverse lookup of data that may exist within SystemDiscoveryArchive that no longer exists within Configuration Manager. If found, a DeletedDate field is updated. This allows you to report on systems added to and removed from Configuration Manager without making any revisions to the Configuration Manager database!

5.   To populate the SystemDiscoveryArchive table for the first time, within **SQL Server Agent Jobs**, select and right-click **System Data Archive Process**, and then select the **Start Job at Step** option. When complete, close the resulting dialog box.

System Data Reports

Now that the framework is in place to capture data added to and removed from Configuration Manager, the final step is importing the reports. There are two reports that have been created for this purpose. The first report is a high-level summary report showing system counts or data added or deleted per day. The second report is a more detailed drilldown report triggered by clicking on hyperlinks from the parent report; to retrieve more information regarding records added or deleted.

To this point, you have learned how to create and publish reports to SSRS with Report Builder and SQL Server Data Tools. In this section, you learn:

- How to import reports directly into SSRS

- How to manually create a data source name (DSN) to access the CMMonitor database

- How to map the imported reports to the newly created DSN

Import the Custom Reports

In this guide, I assume you have copied the book sample files to C:\Setup on PC0001.

1. On **PC0001**, log on as **VIAMONSTRA\Administrator**.

2. Start **Internet Explorer**, and enter **http://cm01.corp.viamonstra.com/reports**.

3. Double-click the **ConfigMgr_PS1** folder, and then locate and double-click the **PracticalReports** folder.

4. In the **SSRS toolbar**, click the **Upload File** button.

5. For the **File to upload**, click **Browse**. Browse to and select **C:\Setup\Chapter8\System Data Detail.rdl**. Then click **Open**, and click **OK** to import the report.

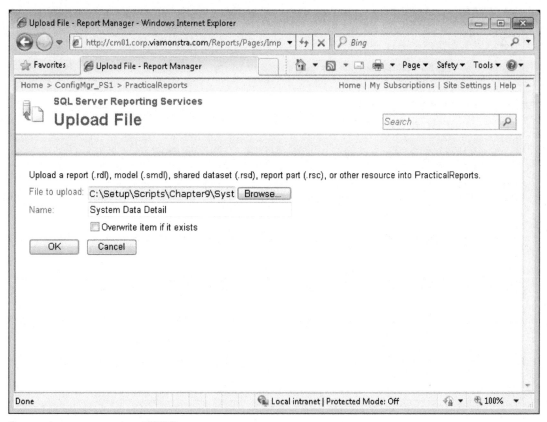

Importing a report into SSRS.

6. Repeat the report **Upload File** process for **C:\Setup\Chapter8\System Data Summary.rdl**.

You should now have the two new reports (System Data Summary and System Data Detail) in the PracticalReports folder.

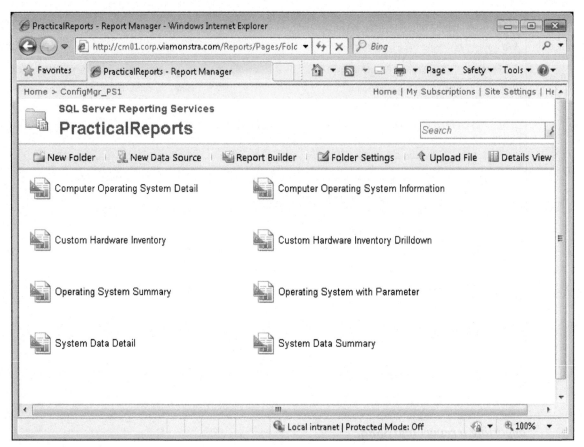

SSRS—System data reports.

7.   Stay in the **PracticalReports** folder and proceed to the next section.

Manually Create a Data Source Name

Any time you need to access a different database, you need to create a DSN. It acts as a connector from the report to the underlying database, sending queries to the database and receiving results for the report.

1. In **Internet Explorer**, while in the **PracticalReports** folder, from the toolbar, click **New Data Source**.

2. You next perform the following steps:

   a. For **Name**, type **CMMonitorDSN**.

   b. For **Connection string**, type

   ```
   Persist Security Info=False;Initial Catalog=CMMonitor;Data
   Source=CM01.corp.viamonstra.com;
   ```

   c. Complete the following options **Credentials stored securely in the report server** options:

      i. For **User name**, type **VIAMONSTRA\CM_SR**.

      ii. For **Password**, type **P@ssw0rd**.

      iii. Select the **Use as Windows Credentials when connecting to the data source** check box.

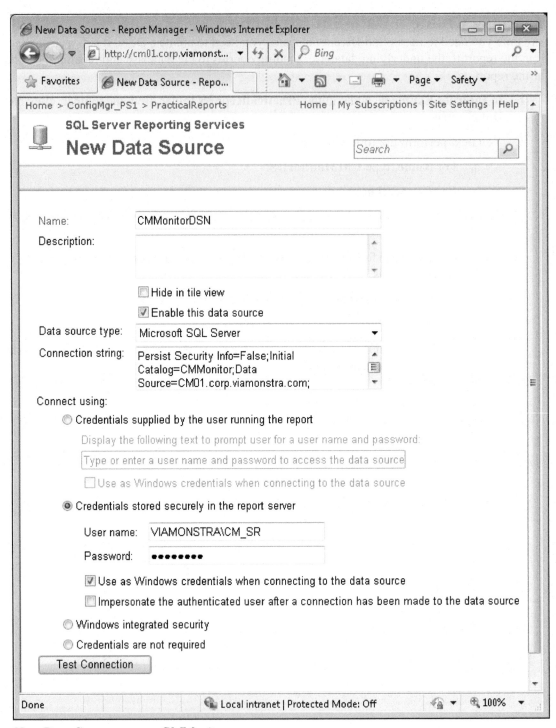

New Data Source name—CMMonitor.

3. Near the bottom of window, click **Test Connection**. You should receive a failure message. Leave the **New Data Source** window open. *Do not close it!*

Note: The **VIAMONSTRA\CM_SR** account that was entered does not have sufficient permissions to access the CMMonitor database.

---

4. To correct the permissions issue, open **SSMS**, expand the top **Security** node, and then expand the **Logins** node. Select user login **VIAMONSTRA\CM_SR**, and right-click **Properties.**

5. In **Login Properties**, in the left pane, select **User Mapping**. Then, under **Users mapped to this login**, in the **CMMonitor** row, select the check box to enable **Map**. Under **Database role membership for CMMonitor**, enable **db_datareader**. Then click **OK**.

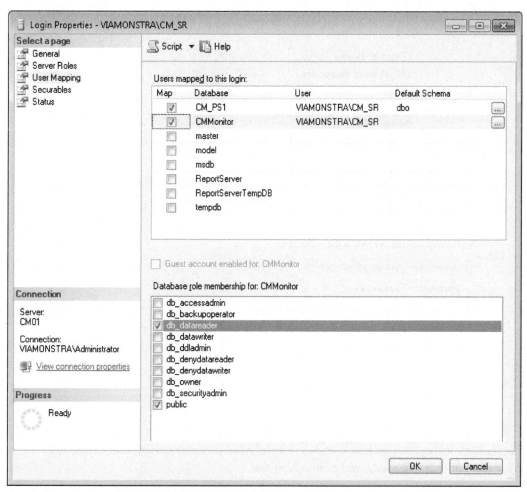

Login Properties—The VIAMONSTRA/CM_SR account.

179

6. Returning to the **New Data Source** window, click **Test Connection**. You should see a message below the Test Connection button: "Connection created successfully".

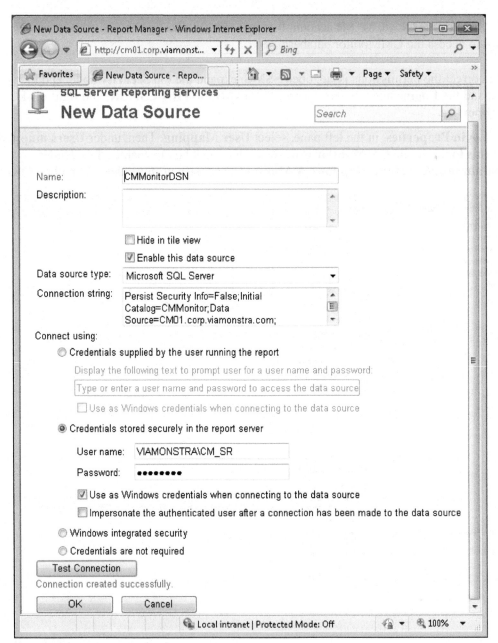

New Data Source—A successful connection test.

7. Click **OK** to save the **DSN**.

Map the Report to the New DSN

Now that you have imported the reports and created the DSN, the remaining step is to associate the reports to the DSN.

1. On **PC0001**, log on as **VIAMONSTRA\Administrator**.

2. Start **Internet Explorer**, and enter **http://cm01.corp.viamonstra.com/reports**.

3. Double-click the **ConfigMgr_PS1** folder, and then locate and double-click the **PracticalReports** folder.

4. To the right of the report named **System Data Summary**, select the drop-down menu and select **Manage**.

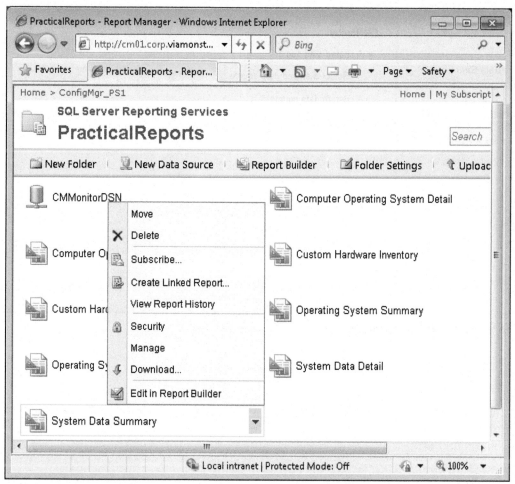

SSRS—Manage reports.

181

5. In the left pane, click **Data Sources**. Note that there is an error message indicating "The shared data source reference is no longer valid".

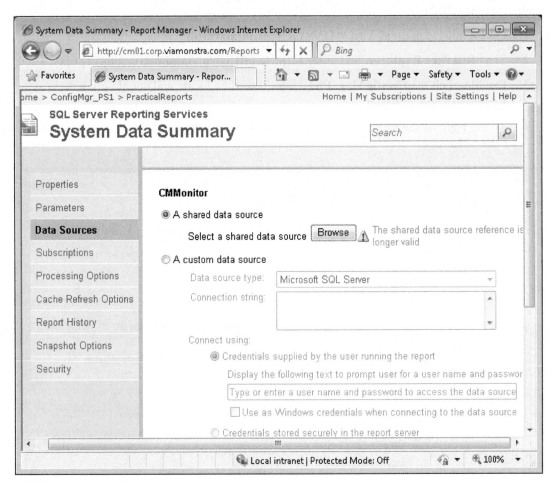

SSRS—An invalid data source.

6. Click **Browse**. Expand **ConfigMgr_PS1**, locate and expand the **PracticalReports** folder, and then select **CMMonitorDSN**.

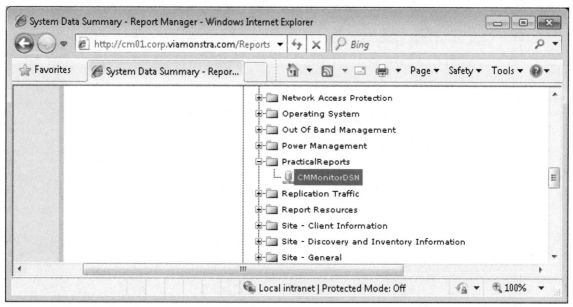

SSRS—Selecting the DSN.

7. Scroll to the bottom, and click **OK**. Then click **Apply** to save changes.

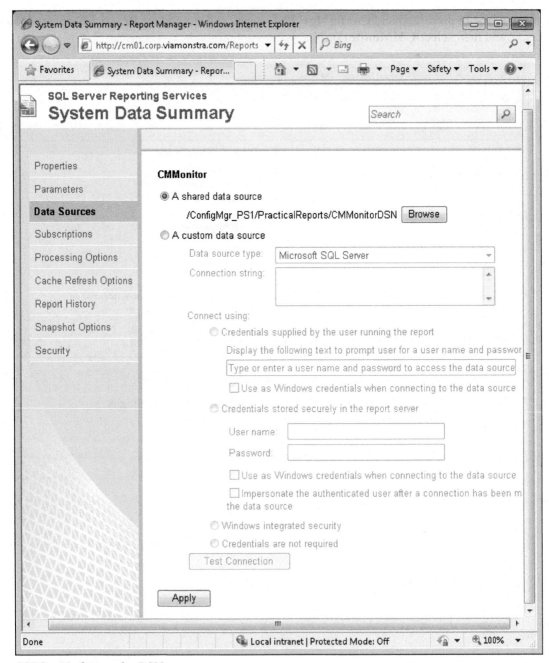

SSRS—Updating the DSN.

8. Repeat steps 4–7 for the **System Data Detail** report.

9. From the SSRS **PracticalReports** folder, click to run **System Data Summary**.

10. Note that no data is displayed. This report is designed (by default) to return results for the last seven days, for systems added and deleted. Change the **To Date** to tomorrow, and click **View Report**.

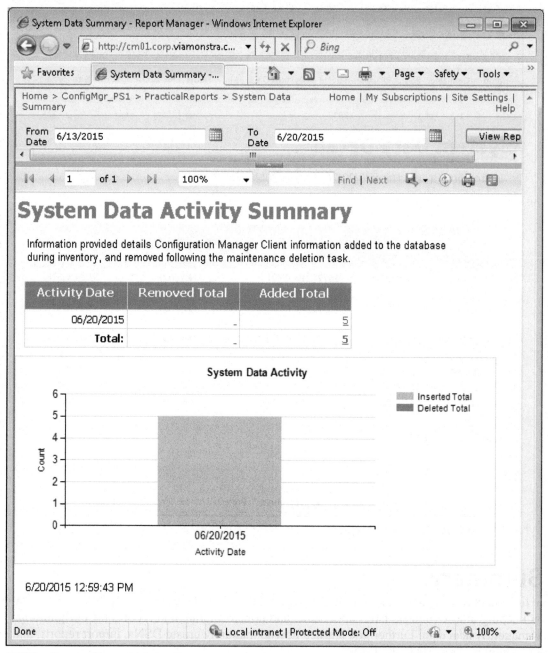

SSRS—System Data Activity Summary report.

11. Click the **Added Total** line to invoke the System Data Detail report. Observe the detail regarding the systems added (or deleted) during this period.

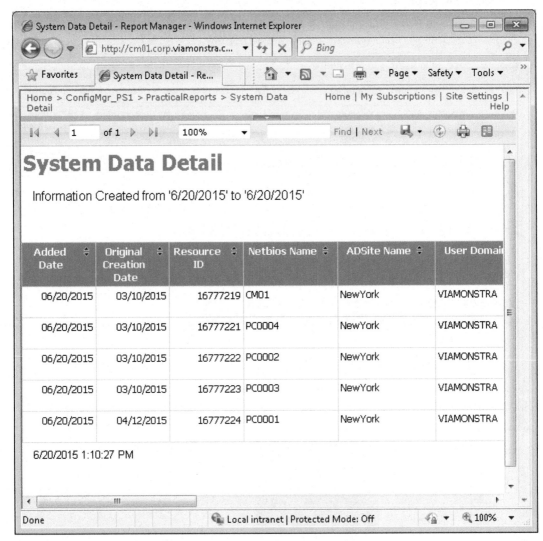

SSRS—System Data Detail report.

Summary

In this chapter, you have learned how to create a custom database, how to optimize your database by keeping indexes and statistics up-to-date, and how to capture and report on Configuration Manager System data. Further you learned how to manually create DSNs, import reports, and map those imported reports to the DSN.

Chapter 9

Report Subscriptions

In this chapter, you learn how to create reports subscriptions using native SQL Server Reporting Services functionality. I cover permissions required for report subscriptions and how to properly configure reports for subscriptions to be delivered via email or to a file share.

SQL Server Reporting Services has many nice features. Perhaps one of the most powerful is the ability to create subscriptions to previously created reports. Subscriptions can take the form of data-driven, email, file-share delivery, and/or integration with SharePoint.

Step-by-Step Guide Requirements

If you want to follow the step-by-step guides in this chapter, you need a lab environment configured as outlined in Chapter 1, have configured Reporting Services in Chapter 2, and have installed SQL Server Management Studio on PC0001 in Chapter 3. In this chapter, you use the following virtual machines:

DC01

CM01

PC0001

The VMs used in this chapter.

You should have the following software installed on PC0001:

- SQL Server Management Studio
- SQL Server Data Tools

Note: If you used the setup process for SQL Server Management Studio in Chapter 3, you are all set! You need the reports that were created in Chapter 6.

Report Subscriptions Background

While primarily intended for Configuration Manager 2012 administrators, this information applies to anyone using SSRS subscriptions.

Subscription Overview

A *subscription* is a standing request to deliver a report at a specific time or in response to an event, and then to have that report presented in a way that you define. Subscriptions provide an alternative to running a report on demand. On-demand reporting requires that you actively select the report each time you want to view it. In contrast, subscriptions can be used to schedule and then automate the delivery of a report.

Standard and Data-Driven Subscriptions

Reporting Services supports two kinds of subscriptions: standard and data-driven. Standard subscriptions are created and managed by individual users. A standard subscription consists of static values that cannot be varied during subscription processing. For each standard subscription, there is exactly one set of report presentation options, delivery options, and report parameters.

Data-driven subscriptions are dynamic in that the presentation, delivery, and parameter values are retrieved at runtime from a data source. You might use data-driven subscriptions if you have a very large recipient list or if you want to vary report output for each recipient. To use data-driven subscriptions, you must have expertise in building queries and an understanding of how parameters are used. Report server administrators typically create and manage these subscriptions. For more information, see Data-Driven Subscriptions in the Resources section.

Email, File Share, and Custom Delivery

Subscriptions use delivery extensions to determine how to distribute a report and in what format. When a user creates a subscription, he or she can choose one of the available delivery extensions to determine how the report is delivered. Reporting Services includes support for email delivery and delivery to a file share. Developers can create additional delivery extensions to route reports to other locations. Another delivery method is called the *null-delivery provider*. This method is not available to users. Null delivery is used by administrators to improve report server performance by preloading the cache.

Parts of a Subscription

A subscription consists of the following parts:

- A report that can run unattended (that is, a report that uses stored credentials or no credentials)

- A delivery method (for example, email) and settings for the mode of delivery (such as an email address)

- A rendering extension to present the report in a specific format

Conditions for Processing the Subscription

Usually, the conditions for running a report are time-based and expressed as an event. For example, you may want to run a particular report every Tuesday at 3:00 P.M. GMT. However, if the report runs as a snapshot, you can specify that the subscription runs whenever the snapshot is refreshed.

Parameters Used When Running the Report

Parameters are optional and are specified only for reports that accept parameter values. Because a subscription is typically user-owned, the parameter values that are specified vary from subscription to subscription. For example, sales managers for different divisions use parameters that return data for their division. All parameters must have a value explicitly defined, or have a valid default value.

Subscription information is stored with individual reports in a report server database. You cannot manage subscriptions separately from the report to which they are associated. Note that subscriptions cannot be extended to include descriptions, other custom text, or other elements. Subscriptions can contain only the items listed earlier.

Let's check that you have the prerequisites in place for subscriptions to be created:

- Reporting Services is installed and running.

- SQL Server Agent is running—SQL Server Agent is the scheduling agent, so it must be functional.

- SMTP is installed and configured.

- Using Reporting Services Configuration Manager, you have defined valid email settings (this will be the sender email).

> **Note**: Either local or remote SMTP configuration can be used. Please see the "Resources" section of this chapter for more information on this topic.

As mentioned earlier in this chapter, SQL Server subscriptions require the SQL Server Agent to be running in order to schedule the subscriptions. Schedules can be created as shared or individual schedules. Shared schedules can be reused for multiple reports, or created per report as an individual schedule.

Report Subscription Permissions

Schedules are created based on membership in specific SQL Server roles. The most common roles used are the System Administrator and Content Manager roles, in that, either role can manage all available subscriptions. By using the other predefined roles defined below, it is possible to limit specific report subscriptions to specific users.

If you are using predefined roles, users who are Content Managers and System Administrators can create and manage any schedule. If you use custom role assignments, the role assignment must include tasks that support scheduled operations.

SSRS—Report Task Matrix		
To do this	*Include this task*	*Predefined roles*
Create, modify, or delete shared schedules	Manage shared schedules	System Administrator
Select shared schedules	View shared schedules	System User
Create, modify, or delete report-specific schedules in a user-defined subscription	Manage individual subscriptions	Browser, Report Builder, My Reports, Content Manager
Create, modify, or delete report-specific schedules for all other scheduled operations	Manage report history, manage all subscriptions, manage reports	Content Manager

Creating the Report Subscription

In this scenario, you create report subscriptions using the SSRS Report Manager. This interface works for all reports. While it is possible to create subscriptions from the Configuration Manager console, the console can manage only the Configuration Manager reports. This topic provides instructions for creating a report-delivery subscription sent to a file share.

To begin, you need the following prerequisites:

- You need to define a server UNC share to send the report data.

- You must have view access to the report.

- You are a member of one or more of the appropriate role-based access control (RBAC) roles listed in the preceding "Report Subscription Permissions" section.

- The report must have stored credentials, or require no credentials at the time of execution. Reports that use impersonated or delegated credentials to connect to an external data source cannot be subscribed.

To subscribe to a report, the report DSN must be configured to use stored credentials or no credentials.

Real World Note: I recommend creating a new data source that is used for subscriptions that will use a stored account to execute the subscribed report. Use an account that has the minimum rights/ability to invoke reports. Do not use an administrator account for this operation!

In these steps, I assume that you have downloaded the book sample files, and copied them to C:\Setup on CM01.

1. On **CM01**, log on as **VIAMONSTRA\Administrator**.

2. Open an elevated **PowerShell** prompt, and create a **Configuration Manager** reporting data folder structure by running the following command:

   ```
   C:\Setup\Scripts\Create-ConfigMgrFoldersReports.ps1
   ```

3. On **PC0001**, log on as **VIAMONSTRA\Administrator**.

4. Because you need to create a subscription for the **Computer Operating System Detail** report, you need to determine whether the DSN is correctly configured.

5. Start **Internet Explorer**, and enter **http://cm01.corp.viamonstra.com/reports**.

6. Double-click the **ConfigMgr_PS1** folder, and then locate and double-click the **PracticalReports** folder.

7. Select the **Computer Operating System Detail** report, click the drop-down menu, and then click **Manage**.

8. In the left pane, click **Data Sources**. Note the DSN name (**CMPS1**) and the path (**/Data Sources/CMPS1**).

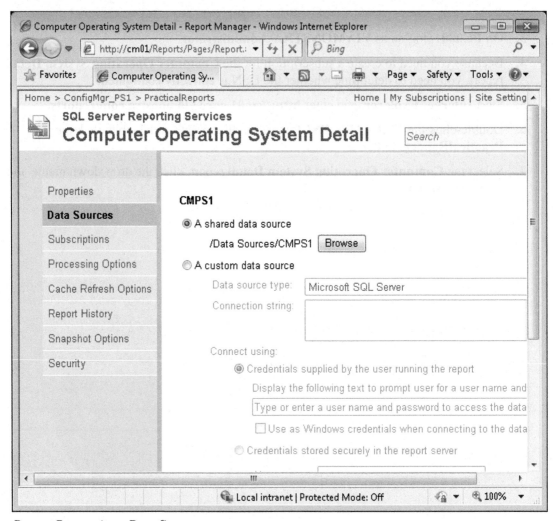

Report Properties—Data Sources.

> **Note**: Now, you need to check the DSN for the proper credential requirements. This is a one-time setup.

9. In the upper left, click **Home**. Then, click the **Data Sources** folder.

10. Select the **CMPS1** DSN, click the drop-down menu, and then click **Manage**.

11. Select the **Credentials stored securely in the report server** option, configure the following settings:

    a.   For **User name**, type **VIAMONSTRA\CM_SR**.

b. For **Password**, type **P@ssw0rd**.

c. Select the **Use as Windows Credentials when connecting to the data source** check box.

d. Click **Apply**.

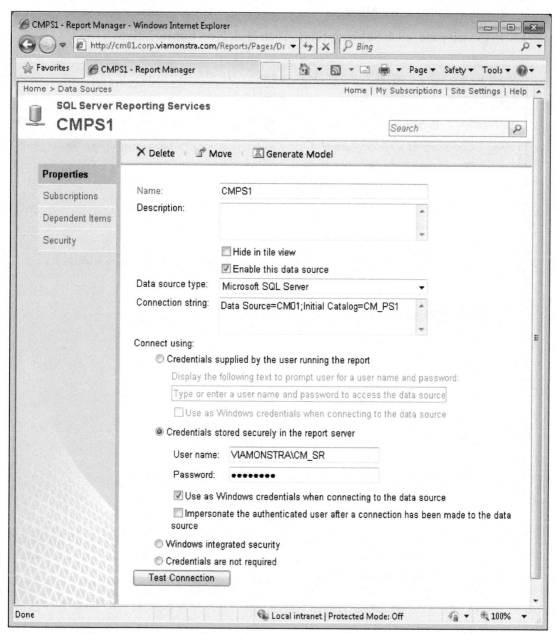

Data Sources—Credentials required for subscriptions.

Real World Note: The connection string varies depending on your database name. The important part is the section that includes "Credentials stored securely on the report server" and the "Use as windows credentials when connecting to the data source" check box.

12. Navigate back to the **Computer Operating System Detail** report, click the drop-down menu, and then select **Manage.**

13. In the left pane, click **Subscriptions**. Then click **New Subscription**.

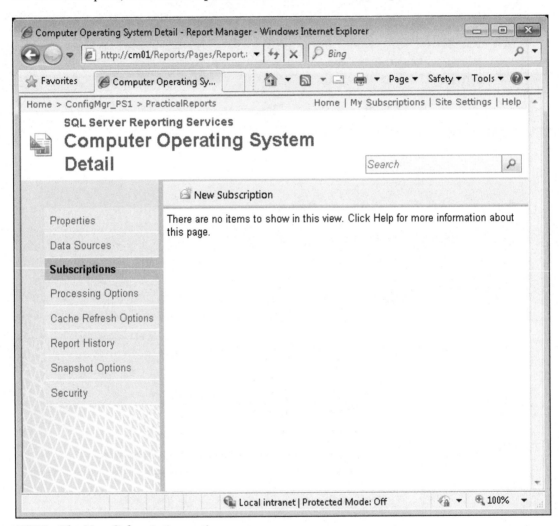

SSRS—The New Subscription option.

14. For the **Subscription** options, perform the following tasks:

    a.   For **Delivered by**, select **Windows File Share**.

    b.   For **Path**, type **\\CM01\Reports**.

    c.   For **Render Format**, select **Word**.

Note: There are 12 different report output formats available!

    d.   For **Credentials used to access the file share**:

        i.   For **User name**, type **VIAMONSTRA\CM_SR**.

        ii.   For **Password**, type **P@ssw0rd**.

    e.   For **Overwrite options**, select **Increment file names as newer versions are available**.

    Below **Subscription Processing Options**, note by default the report will run once each Monday at 8:00 AM.

Note: The schedule can be revised with the Select Schedule button.

15. Then, click **OK**.

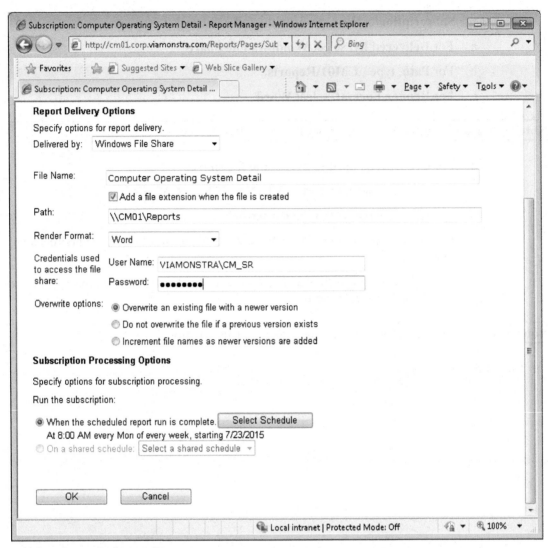

SSRS—Report Delivery Options.

16. Optionally, as a test, using **steps 12–15**, create one more additional subscription. Using the **Select Schedule** button, on the **Schedule details** page, chose **Once**, and then enter a **One-time Schedule** to occur in 10 minutes from the present time.

Real World Note: The site server may be in a different time zone, so verify the local time at the site server before proceeding! Reports can have multiple subscriptions for different purposes and deliver methods.

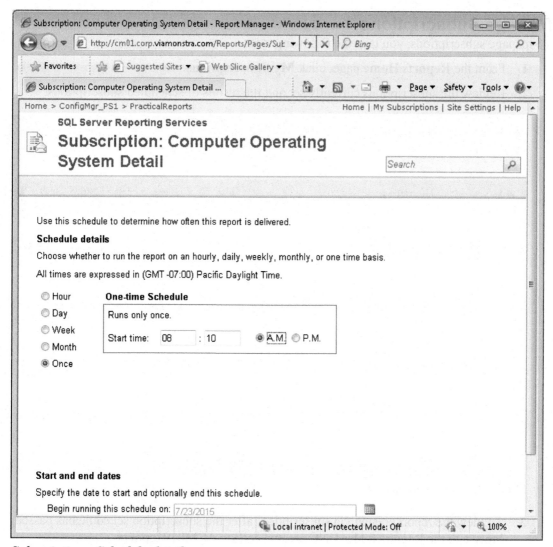

Subscription—Schedule details.

17. Click **OK**.

Manage Subscriptions

To manage subscriptions, you take the following steps:

1. From the **Reports Home** page, click **My Subscriptions**.

2. Review the subscriptions currently set and the results of scheduled subscriptions.

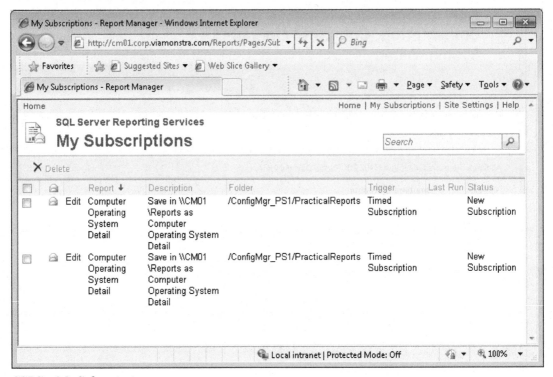

SSRS—My Subscriptions.

3. To view the report created via subscription, after the subscription schedule has passed, browse to the Reports folder UNC created earlier: **\\CM01\Reports**.

    You should see one or more reports in that location.

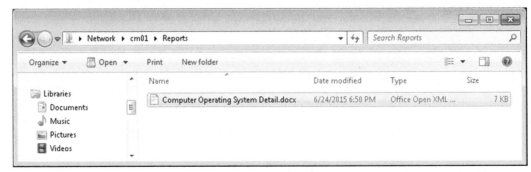

Reports folder—Completed reports.

Summary

In this chapter, you have learned how to create and manage report subscriptions. You now have the background on the various elements of subscriptions and required permissions.

Experiment with creating subscriptions using SMTP for email. With emailed subscriptions, you have two options: sending the report as an attachment, or sending the email with a link to the report located on a server UNC. The latter approach is far more efficient, and a history of scheduled reports can be maintained in one location.

Resources

The following resources are useful articles from Microsoft and other community sources as appropriate.

Configure a Report Server for E-Mail Delivery
https://msdn.microsoft.com/en-us/library/ms159155(v=sql.110).aspx

Configure a Report Server Database Connection (Native Mode)
https://msdn.microsoft.com/en-us/library/ms159133(v=sql.110).aspx

Data-Driven Subscriptions
https://msdn.microsoft.com/en-us/library/ms159150(v=sql.110).aspx

How to Subscribe to a Report (Management Studio)
https://technet.microsoft.com/en-us/library/ms157386(v=sql.105).aspx

Appendix A

Using the Hydration Kit to Build the PoC Environment

Hydration is the concept of using a deployment solution, like MDT 2013, to do a fully automated build of an entire lab, or proof-of-concept environment. This appendix is here to help you quickly spin up a lab environment that matches up with all the guides you use in this book.

I recommend using Hyper-V in Windows Server 2012 R2 as your virtual platform, but I have tested the hydration kit on the following virtual platforms:

- Hyper-V in Windows 8.1 and Windows Server 2012 R2
- VMware Workstation 11.0
- VMware ESXi 5.5

As you learned in Chapter 1, to set up a virtual environment with all the servers and clients, you need a host with at least 16 GB of RAM, even though 32 GB RAM is recommended. Either way, make sure you are using SSD drives for your storage. A single 480 GB SSD is enough to run all the scenarios in this book.

> **Real World Note:** Don't go cheap on the disk drive. If using a normal laptop or desktop when doing the step-by-step guides in this book, please, please, please use a SSD drive for your virtual machines. Using normal spindle-based disks are just too slow for a decent lab and test environment. Also, please note that most laptops support at least 16 GB RAM these days, even if many vendors does not update their specifications with this information.

The Base Servers

Using the hydration kit, you build the following list of servers.

New York Site Servers (192.168.1.0/24)

- **DC01.** Domain Controller, DNS, and DHCP
- **CM01.** Member Server

The Base Clients

In addition to the servers, you also use a few clients throughout the book guides.

New York Site Clients (192.168.1.0/24)

- **PC0001.** Windows 7 SP1 Enterprise x64

- **PC0002.** Windows 7 SP1 Enterprise x64

- **PC0003.** Windows 8.1 Enterprise x64

- **PC0004.** Windows 8.1 Enterprise x64

Internet Access

As you learned in Chapter 1, the guides in this book do not require you to have Internet access on the virtual machines, but it's quite handy configuring them for it. I recommend using either a virtual router (running in a VM) to provide Internet access to your lab and test VMs, or enabling Internet Connection Sharing (ICS) on the host. If you go the virtual router approach, you can use either the Vyatta / VyOS (Vyatta community fork) routers, or a Windows Server 2012 R2 virtual machine with routing configured.

> **Real World Note:** For detailed guidance on setting up a virtual router for your lab environment, see this article: http://tinyurl.com/usingvirtualrouter.

Setting Up the Hydration Environment

To enable you to quickly set up the servers and clients used for the step-by-step guides in this book, I provide you with a hydration kit (part of the book sample files) that will build all the servers and clients. The sample files are available for download at http://deploymentfundamentals.com.

How Does the Hydration Kit Work?

The hydration kit that you download is just a folder structure and some scripts. The scripts help you create the MDT 2013 Lite Touch offline media (big ISO), and the folder structure is there for you to add your own software and licenses when applicable. You can use trial versions for the lab software, as well. The overview steps are the following:

1. Download the needed software.

2. Install MDT 2013 Lite Touch and Windows ADK 8.1.

3. Create a MDT 2013 deployment share.

4. Populate the folder structure with your media and any license information.

5. Generate the MDT 2013 media item (big ISO).

6. Create a few virtual machines, boot them on the media item, select what servers they should become, and about two hours later you have the lab environment ready to go.

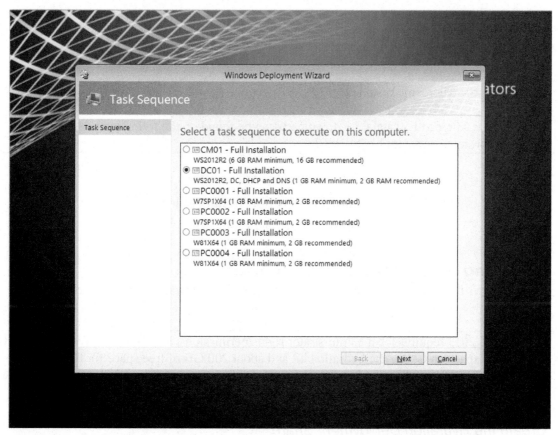

The end result: You boot a VM from the ISO and simply select which server to build.

Preparing the Downloads Folder

These steps should be performed on the Windows machine that you use to manage Hyper-V or VMware. If you are using Hyper-V or VMware Workstation, this machine also can be the host machine.

Download the Software

1. On the Windows machine that you use to manage Hyper-V or VMware, create the **C:\Downloads** folder.

2. Download the following mandatory software to the **C:\Downloads** folder:

    o   The book sample files (http://deploymentfundamentals.com)

    o   Windows ADK 8.1 (To download the full ADK, you run adksetup.exe once and select to download the files.)

- o   BGInfo
- o   MDT 2013
- o   Microsoft Visual C++ 2005 SP1 runtimes (both x86 and x64)
- o   Microsoft Visual C++ 2008 SP1 runtimes (both x86 and x64)
- o   Microsoft Visual C++ 2010 SP1 runtimes (both x86 and x64)
- o   Microsoft Visual C++ 2012 SP1 runtimes (both x86 and x64)

Note: All the Microsoft Visual C++ downloads can be found on the following page: http://support.microsoft.com/kb/2019667.

- o   Windows Server 2012 R2 (trial or full version)
- o   Windows 7 SP1 Enterprise x64 (trial or full version)
- o   Windows 8.1 Enterprise x64 (trial or full version)

Preparing the Hydration Environment

The Windows machine that you use to manage Hyper-V or VMware needs to have PowerShell installed.

Note: MDT 2013 requires local administrator rights/permissions. You need to have at least 60 GB of free disk space on C:\ for the hydration kit and about 200 GB of free space for the volume hosting your virtual machines. Also make sure to run all commands from an elevated PowerShell prompt.

Create the Hydration Deployment Share

1.   On the Windows machine that you use to manage Hyper-V or VMware, install **ADK** (**adksetup.exe**) selecting only the following components:

   - o   **Deployment Tools**
   - o   **Windows Preinstallation Environment (Windows PE)**

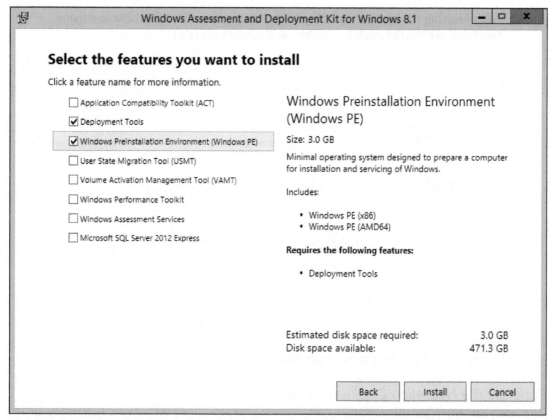

The Windows ADK 8.1 setup.

2. Install **MDT 2013 (MicrosoftDeploymentToolkit2013_x64.msi)** with the default settings.

3. Extract the book sample files and copy the **HydrationCM2012Reporting** folder to **C:**.

    You should now have the following folder containing a few subfolders and PowerShell scripts:

    C:\HydrationCM2012Reporting\Source

4. In an elevated (run as Administrator) **PowerShell** prompt, navigate to the hydration folder by running the following command:

    ```
    Set-Location C:\HydrationCM2012Reporting\Source
    ```

5. Still at the **PowerShell** prompt, with location (working directory) set to **C:\HydrationCM2012Reporting\Source**, create the hydration deployment share by running the following command:

    ```
    .\CreateHydrationDeploymentShare.ps1
    ```

6. After creating the hydration deployment share, review the added content using **Deployment Workbench** (available on the **Start screen**).

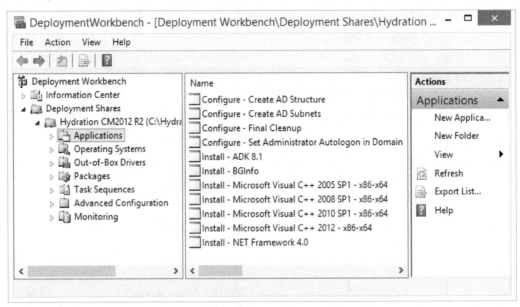

Deployment Workbench with the readymade applications listed.

Populate the Hydration Deployment Share with the Setup Files

In these steps, you copy the installation files to the correct target folder in the hydration structure:

1. Copy the Windows ADK 8.1 installation files to the following folder:

   C:\HydrationCM2012Reporting\DS\Applications\Install - ADK\Source

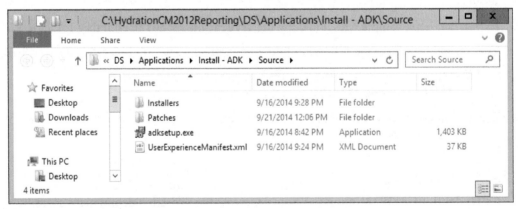

The Windows ADK 8.1 files copied.

2. Copy the **BGInfo** file (**bginfo.exe**) to the following folder:

   C:\HydrationCM2012Reporting\DS\Applications\Install - BGInfo\Source

3. Copy the **Microsoft Visual C++ 2005 SP1 x86** and **Microsoft Visual C++ 2005 SP1 x64** installation files (**vcredist_x86.exe and vcredist_x64.exe**) to the following folder:

   C:\HydrationCM2012Reporting\DS\Applications
   Install - Microsoft Visual C++ 2005 SP1 - x86-x64\Source

4. Copy the **Microsoft Visual C++ 2008 SP1 x86** and **Microsoft Visual C++ 2008 SP1 x64** installation files (**vcredist_x86.exe and vcredist_x64.exe**) to the following folder:

   C:\HydrationCM2012Reporting\DS\Applications
   Install - Microsoft Visual C++ 2008 SP1 - x86-x64\Source

5. Copy the **Microsoft Visual C++ 2010 SP1 x86** and **Microsoft Visual C++ 2010 SP1 x64** installation files (**vcredist_x86.exe and vcredist_x64.exe**) to the following folder:

   C:\HydrationCM2012Reporting\DS\Applications
   Install - Microsoft Visual C++ 2010 SP1 - x86-x64\Source

6. Copy the **Microsoft Visual C++ 2012 x86** and **Microsoft Visual C++ 2012 x64** installation files (**vcredist_x86.exe and vcredist_x64.exe**) to the following folder:

   C:\HydrationCM2012Reporting\DS\Applications
   Install - Microsoft Visual C++ 2012 - x86-x64\Source

7. Copy the **Windows Server 2012 R2** installation files (the content of the ISO, not the actual ISO) to the following folder:

   C:\HydrationCM2012Reporting\DS\Operating Systems\WS2012R2

8. Copy the **Windows 7 SP1 Enterprise x64** installation files (again, the content of the ISO, not the actual ISO) to the following folder:

   C:\HydrationCM2012Reporting\DS\Operating Systems\W7SP1X64

9. Copy the **Windows 8.1 Enterprise x64** installation files (again, the content of the ISO, not the actual ISO) to the following folder:

   C:\HydrationCM2012Reporting\DS\Operating Systems\W81X64

Create the Hydration ISO (MDT 2013 Update Offline Media Item)

1. Using **Deployment Workbench** (available on the **Start screen**), expand **Deployment Shares**, and expand **Hydration CM2012 R2**.

2. Review the various nodes. The **Applications**, **Operating Systems**, and **Task Sequences** nodes should all have some content in them.

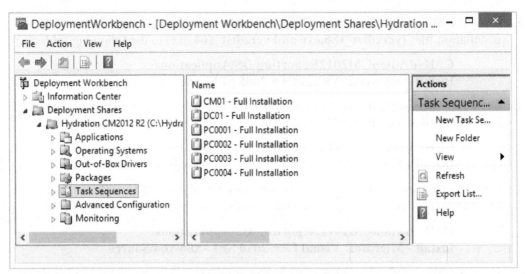

The Hydration deployment share, listing all task sequences.

3. Expand the **Advanced Configuration** node, and then select the **Media** node.

4. In the right pane, right-click the **MEDIA001** item, and select **Update Media Content**.

> **Note:** The most common reason for failures in the hydration kit are related to antivirus software preventing the ISO from being generated correctly. If you see any errors in the update media content process, disable (or uninstall) your antivirus software, and then try the update again. Anyway, the media update will take a while to run, a perfect time for a coffee break. ☺

After the media update, you have a big ISO (HydrationCM2012Reporting.iso) in the C:\HydrationCM2012Reporting\ISO folder. The ISO will be between 13 and 15 GB in size depending on which Windows media you have been using. (You have probably noticed that Microsoft offers ISO files with updates already installed, and these ISO files are larger.)

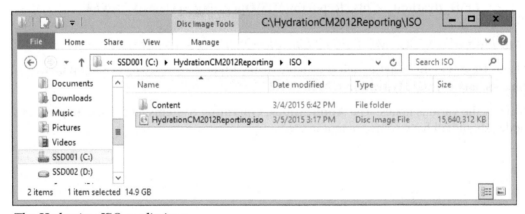

The Hydration ISO media item.

Deploying the New York Site VMs

In these steps, you deploy and configure the virtual machines for the New York site.

Deploy DC01

This is the primary domain controller used in the environment, and it also runs DNS and DHCP.

1. Using **Hyper-V Manager** or **VMware Sphere**, create a virtual machine with the following settings:

   a.   Name: **DC01**

   b.   Memory: **1 GB** (minimum, 2 GB recommended)

   c.   Hard drive: **100 GB** (dynamic disk)

   d.   Network: The virtual network for the New York site

   e.   Image file (ISO):
       C:\HydrationCM2012Reporting\ISO\HydrationCM2012Reporting.iso

   f.   vCPUs: **2**

2. Start the **DC01** virtual machine. After booting from **HydrationCM2012Reporting.iso**, and after WinPE has loaded, select the **DC01** task sequence.

Real World Note: Using a dynamic disk is really useful for a lab and test environment because the host PC uses only the actually consumed space on the virtual hard drive and not the size that you type in like a fixed disk would.

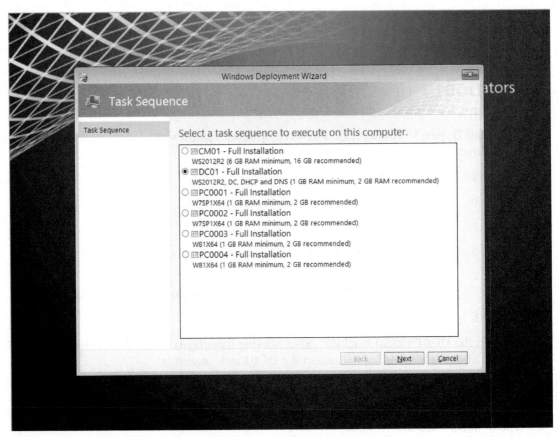

The Task Sequence list showing the hydration task sequences.

3. Wait until the setup is complete and you see the **Hydration completed** message in the final summary. Then leave the **DC01** virtual machine running.

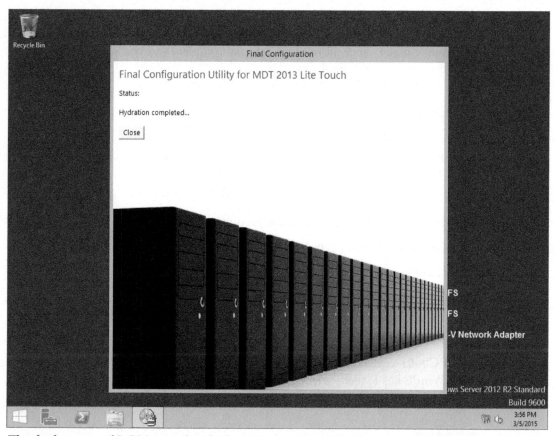

The deployment of DC01 completed, showing the custom final summary screen.

Deploy CM01

CM01 is the server used for Configuration Manager 2012 R2.

1. Using **Hyper-V Manager** or **VMware Sphere**, create a virtual machine with the following settings:

    a. Name: **CM01**

    b. Memory: **6 GB** (minimum, 16 GB recommended)

    c. Hard drive: **100 GB** (dynamic disk)

    d. Network: The virtual network for the New York site

    e. Image file (ISO):
        C:\HydrationCM2012Reporting\ISO\HydrationCM2012Reporting.iso

    f. vCPUs: **2** (minimum, 4 recommended)

2. Make sure the **DC01** virtual machine is running, and then start the **CM01** virtual machine. After booting from **HydrationCM2012Reporting.iso**, and after WinPE has loaded, select the **CM01** task sequence. Wait until the setup is complete and you see the **Hydration completed** message in the final summary.

Deploy PC0001

This is a client running Windows 7 SP1 Enterprise x64 in the domain.

1. Using **Hyper-V Manager** or **VMware Sphere**, create a virtual machine with the following settings:

   a. Name: **PC0001**

   b. Memory: **1 GB** (minimum, 2 GB recommended)

   c. Hard drive: **60 GB** (dynamic disk)

   d. Network: The virtual network for the New York site

   e. Image file (ISO):
   C:\HydrationCM2012Reporting\ISO\HydrationCM2012Reporting.iso

   f. vCPUs: **1** (minimum, 2 recommended)

2. Start the **PC0001** virtual machine. After booting from **HydrationCM2012Reporting.iso**, and after WinPE has loaded, select the **PC0001** task sequence. Wait until the setup is complete and you see the **Hydration completed** message in the final summary.

Deploy PC0002

This is an extra client running Windows 7 SP1 Enterprise x64 in the domain.

1. Using **Hyper-V Manager** or **VMware Sphere**, create a virtual machine with the following settings:

   a. Name: **PC0002**

   b. Memory: **2 GB**

   c. Hard drive: **60 GB** (dynamic disk)

   d. Network: The virtual network for the New York site

   e. Image file (ISO):
   C:\HydrationCM2012Reporting\ISO\HydrationCM2012Reporting.iso

   f. vCPUs: **1** (minimum, 2 recommended)

2. Start the **PC0002** virtual machine. After booting from **HydrationCM2012Reporting.iso**, and after WinPE has loaded, select the **PC0002** task sequence. Wait until the setup is complete and you see the **Hydration completed** message in the final summary.

Deploy PC0003

This is an extra client running Windows 8.1 Enterprise x64 in the domain.

1. Using **Hyper-V Manager** or **VMware Sphere**, create a virtual machine with the following settings:

    a. Name: **PC0003**

    b. Memory: **2 GB**

    c. Hard drive: **60 GB** (dynamic disk)

    d. Network: The virtual network for the New York site

    e. Image file (ISO):
       C:\HydrationCM2012Reporting\ISO\HydrationCM2012Reporting.iso

    f. vCPUs: **1** (minimum, 2 recommended)

2. Start the **PC0003** virtual machine. After booting from **HydrationCM2012Reporting.iso**, and after WinPE has loaded, select the **PC0003** task sequence. Wait until the setup is complete and you see the **Hydration completed** message in the final summary.

Deploy PC0004

This is an extra client running Windows 8.1 Enterprise x64 in the domain.

1. Using **Hyper-V Manager** or **VMware Sphere**, create a virtual machine with the following settings:

    a. Name: **PC0004**

    b. Memory: **2 GB**

    c. Hard drive: **60 GB** (dynamic disk)

    d. Network: The virtual network for the New York site

    e. Image file (ISO):
       C:\HydrationCM2012Reporting\ISO\HydrationCM2012Reporting.iso

    f. vCPUs: **1** (minimum, 2 recommended)

2. Start the **PC0004** virtual machine. After booting from **HydrationCM2012Reporting.iso**, and after WinPE has loaded, select the **PC0004** task sequence. Wait until the setup is complete and you see the **Hydration completed** message in the final summary.

Index

Beyond the Book – Meet the Expert

If you liked Steve's book, you will love to hear him in person.

Live Presentations

Steve frequently speaks at computer industry conferences around the world, such as IT / Dev Connections and Midwest Management Summit (MMS). You also find additional information on his blog:

https://stevethompsonmvp.wordpress.com/

Twitter

Steve also tweets on the following alias: @Steve_TSQL.

CPSIA information can be obtained
at www.ICGtesting.com
Printed in the USA
LVOW02s2139300617

539949LV00002BA/2/P